UNINTENDED CONSEQUENCES OF HUMAN ACTIONS

Elena Ermolaeva
and
Jessica Ross

University Press of America,® Inc.
Lanham · Boulder · New York · Toronto · Plymouth, UK

Copyright © 2011 by
University Press of America,® Inc.
4501 Forbes Boulevard
Suite 200
Lanham, Maryland 20706
UPA Acquisitions Department (301) 459-3366

Estover Road
Plymouth PL6 7PY
United Kingdom

All rights reserved
Printed in the United States of America
British Library Cataloging in Publication Information Available

Library of Congress Control Number: 2010938993
ISBN: 978-0-7618-5445-6 (paperback : alk. paper)

∞™ The paper used in this publication meets the minimum
requirements of American National Standard for Information
Sciences—Permanence of Paper for Printed Library Materials,
ANSI Z39.48-1992

To Umi

Contents

Preface	vii
Chapter 1 Classical Giants on Consequences of Human Actions	1
1.1 Niccolo Machiavelli	1
1.2 Giambattista Vico	3
1.3 Adam Smith	5
1.4 Wilhelm Wundt	6
1.5 Vilfredo Pareto	7
1.6 Max Weber	9
1.7 Graham Wallas	10
Chapter 2 Gender and Family	13
2.1 History of Family Law	13
2.1.1 John Milton, England, 1643	13
2.1.2 No-Fault Divorce Law, USA, 1970	13
2.2 Genocide in Rwanda on Women in Parliament, 1994	16
2.3 Demographic Change in Japan on Women in Education, 2003—	17
2.4 Honor Killing and Suicide, Western Europe, 2005—	18
2.5 Globalization, Women's Labor Force Participation, and Feminization of Migration	19
Chapter 3 Race and Ethnicity	23
3.1 The Allotment Act of 1887	23
3.2 Indian Reorganization Act (IRA) of 1934	24
3.3 Land Ownership and African American Class Divide	24
3.4 The Jim Crow, White Violence, Civil Rights Act of 1964, and the Role of Television Coverage	25
3.5 Outsourcing Affirmative Action	27
3.6 Invasion in Iraq (2003—) and Sunnis / Shi'ites war	28

Chapter 4 Schools — **31**
  4.1 Opening of Higher Education to Women, USA, 19th century — 31
  4.2 Promise Scholarship, WV, 2002— — 32
  4.3 No Child Left Behind Act, USA, 2002— — 33
  4.4 Centennial "Celebration" of the System of Tracking — 33

Chapter 5 Health Care and Delivery — **37**
  5.1 The Americans with Disabilities Act of 1990 — 37
  5.2 Deinstitutionalization — 38
  5.3 De-industrialization and Obesity — 40

Chapter 6 Government — **43**
  6.1 Welfare Reforms of the 1990s — 43
  6.2 West Virginia and the New Deal — 45
  6.3 China's One Child Policy (1979) on Imbalance of Genders — 47
  6.4 Zimbabwe Land Redistribution of 1990s and 2000 — 48
  6.5 Changes in the Teachers Retirement Systems (TRS) since 1991 (West Virginia) — 49
  6.6 Annexation of Unincorporated Areas (West Virginia) — 51
  6.7 Congressional and State Legislative Redistricting (West Virginia) — 52

Chapter 7 Environment — **55**
  7.1 Release of Domestic European rabbits in Australia in 1859 — 55
  7.2 Fence Construction Along US-Mexican Border — 57
  7.3 Electronic Waste (E-waste) — 58
  7.4 Mountaintop Removal — 60
  7.5 Global Warming — 61
  7.6 Use of Wind Turbines and Wind Energy — 63
  7.7 Introduction of Hybrid Cars and the Use of Ethanol as a Fuel — 64
  7.8 Daylight Saving Time (DST) — 67

Chapter 8 Crime and Crime Control. Drug Use — **71**
  8.1 Cracking Down on Illegal Immigration — 71
  8.2 Megan's Law — 73
  8.3 Legalizing Abortion — 74
  8.4 Amendment 18 (1919) and Alcohol Prohibition — 75
  8.5 The "Three Strikes" Law — 77

Chapter 9 Conclusion. Looking Down the Road — **81**

About the Authors — **87**

Preface

"Never use the words "unanticipated" and "immediate action" in one sentence," according to the leading character of the movie "Michael Clayton" (2008). There is an urgent need to review a range of possible outcomes of human actions. Our lives provide us with numerous examples of unanticipated, unintended, or even ironic consequences. While some outcomes can be intended and predicted there is a possibility of others, not foreseen, that cannot be dealt with in advance of their appearance.

Because public policy decisions are often made in a hurry in order to find a seemingly effective means to an important end, all angles are not studied with precision. Human fallibility and personal interests play into social structure, therefore making outcomes unpredictable. What may start out as an initiative to make a positive change can easily become an unpopular and corrupted system.

The book continues Robert Merton's tradition of search for unintended consequences which he outlined in his outstanding study "The Unanticipated Consequences of Purposive Social Action" (1936). We provide data (or "case studies") from the nineteenth, twentieth, and the twenty first centuries.

The book is organized into nine chapters. Although many cases do involve actions of governments, we tried to structure the text along the major topical areas of college courses—theory, gender and family, race and ethnicity, schools, health care and delivery, government, environment, crime and crime control. The concluding chapter reviews the attempts to "look down the road" in decision making. There are four to eight case studies in each chapter.

Unintended Consequences of Human Actions includes Critical Thinking Questions at the end of each chapter. The students and readers are asked to

1. Discuss the direction of change. For example, good intentions may lead to negative consequences; something positive may come up as a result of negative conditions; or, the consequence is neither good nor bad but a modification of the previous condition, etc.

3. Discuss the nature of consequences—unintended, unanticipated (both unforeseen), ironic.
4. What went "wrong" and why? Why was the outcome unintended/unanticipated? Was it due to ignorance, error, immediate interest, basic values, intensity of the action, etc.?
5. Discuss the nature of an action—was it unorganized or formally organized?

According to Merton, unforeseen consequences should not be identified with consequences which are necessarily undesirable, or in short, undesired effects are not always undesirable effects. In the book we showed various directions of change—from good intentions to negative consequences (examples from the history of family law); from negative conditions to positive outcomes (genocide in Rwanda and election of women to Parliament); and when the consequence is neither good nor bad but a modification of the previous condition (feminization of migration).

Merton used the word "unanticipated" rather than "unintended" and the word "purposive" is meant to stress that the action under study involves the motives of a human actor. He also acknowledged that "the consequences result from the interplay of the action and the objective situation, the conditions of action." In our collection of case studies we demonstrate consequences of, firstly, purposive actions. An example here is the release of domestic European rabbits in Australia in 1859. Because a particular action is not carried out in a psychological or social vacuum, we also review the consequences at a nexus of purposive actions and objective (structural) situations. The showcase here, as one example, is the Indian Reorganization Act of 1934. Thirdly, we provide examples (but constrain ourselves from providing more) of the consequences of objective, structural situations, assuming that humans are the ultimate architects of structures. The current obesity epidemic is at least partially due to deindustrialization—the disappearance of manufacturing jobs which required physical labor.

We draw a distinction between the terms *unanticipated* and *unintended*. Webster defines anticipation as "a visualization of a future event or state." Intention is defined as "what one intends to do or bring about." Anticipation is not listed as a synonym of intention and intention is describing "little more than what one has in mind to do or bring about." The difference between these two terms lies in the way that an action is preceded by thought, planning, and analysis.

When an idea for an action is generated, the person/people responsible for the idea must determine what action to take in order to accomplish the ultimate goal. This process answers the question of whether a consequence should be termed *unanticipated* or *unintended*. Unintended consequences generally result from concentrated analysis of possible outcomes. When an outcome of an action is recognized as possible and the action occurs, producing this outcome, the consequence may have been unintended, but it was not unanticipated.

Anticipation suggests expectation, or at least acceptance of a possibility. If the possibility has been discovered, then it has been anticipated. Unanticipated consequences often stem from quickly made decisions that ignore some factors of a situation. Unintended consequences, on the other hand, can result from well-analyzed decision making processes.

Just because a possible consequence has been recognized and anticipated does not mean that it is intended if the action is performed. For instance, a fast driver recognizes that s/he runs the risk of wrecking their vehicle. This does not mean, however, that this is the intent of the driver. Consequently, this *anticipated* consequence is *unintended*. Conversely, if for some reason a driver were not aware that an accident was possible, a wreck would be an *unanticipated* consequence.

Unintended consequences result from a decision to accept a consequence as possible, but not necessarily desire it as the goal of an action. Unanticipated consequences result from a failure to explore all possible outcomes, therefore creating a result completely unexpected at the origin of the action. The dichotomy between these differing types of consequences complicates the study of an action's results. These consequences might better be collectively referred to as *incongruent* consequences, referring to the disparity between an action's original purpose and its outcome. This term is helpful because it makes no distinction between consequences that have or have not been realized.

The addition of the term irony to discussion is not without purpose, however, as it offers another classification within the terms of unanticipated and unintended consequences. Webster defines irony as "incongruity between the actual result of a sequence of events and the normal and expected result." Irony cannot be used as a blanket term for incongruent consequences, however. While a consequence may be unanticipated or unintended, it is not always negative. The nature of the term *irony* suggests wit, as if the coincidental nature of the consequence is almost darkly comedic. If the consequence is positive and accepted as such, the situation would not best be described as ironic. Irony also suggests an element of surprise, which is not always present, particularly in *unintended* consequences. Claire Colebrook in the work *Irony in the Work of Philosophy* (2002) suggests that we often use the word "irony" to describe a fateful connection we could not have foreseen. It is as though the gods were playing with us, seeing the unfortunate outcomes of our finite acts. We describe as "ironic" the situation of a manager who loses his job as a result of the very corporate downsizing he set in motion; or we use the word "ironically" to describe infelicitous future outcomes. For example, "Ironically, it was only the day after he decided to cancel his thirty-year-old health insurance policy that he discovered he was terminally ill." To use the word "irony" in this sense is to suggest that we are subject to a fate that cannot be foreseen (ibid).

According to Robert Merton, the most obvious limitation to a correct anticipation of consequences of action is provided by the existing state of knowledge or lack of adequate knowledge.

A second major factor of unexpected consequences of conduct is error. We may err in our appraisal of the present situation, in our inference from this to the future objective situation, in our selection of a course of action, or in the execution of the action chosen. A common fallacy is frequently involved in the too ready assumption that actions which have in the past led to the desired outcomes will continue to do so. Error may also be involved in instances where the actor attends to only one or some of the pertinent aspects of the situation which influence the outcome of the action.

The third type of factor, the "imperious immediacy of interest," refers to instances where the actor's paramount concern with the foreseen immediate consequences excludes the consideration of further or other consequences of the same act.

There is one other circumstance, peculiar to human conduct, which stands in the way of successful social prediction and planning: public predictions of future social developments are frequently not sustained precisely because the prediction has become a new element in the concrete situation, thus tending to change the initial course of developments. Merton offers a concrete social example of Marx's prediction of the progressive concentration of wealth and increasing misery of the masses which did influence the very process predicted. The consequences were the spread of organization of labor, increased consciousness of its unfavorable bargaining position, and the rise of collective bargaining—which slowed up the developments which Marx had predicted.

Merton cautions us that there are two pitfalls to be aware of in considering actions and consequences. The first is the problem of causal imputation, that is, the matter of determining to what extent particular consequences ought to be attributed to particular actions. The problem is exacerbated by the fact that consequences can have a number of causes.

The second pitfall is that of determining the actual purposes of a given action. According to Merton, it is not assumed that in fact social action always involves

> clear-cut, explicit purpose. It may well be that such awareness of purpose is unusual, that the aim of action is more often than not nebulous and lazy. This is certainly the case with habitual action which, though it may originally have been induced by conscious purpose, is characteristically performed without such awareness.

Merton differentiates between two types of actions—*unorganized* and *formally organized*. "The first refers to actions of individuals considered distributively . . . the second when like-minded individuals form as association in order to achieve a common purpose. Unanticipated consequences may follow both types of action."

We hope the readers will develop interest in the topic of unforeseen consequences and, at least occasionally, will catch themselves thinking down the road.[1]

We are thankful to Delegate John Doyle (WV House of Delegates) for his contribution of three case studies about our home state of West Virginia. We both are grateful to the Marshall University Advance program for financial assistance. We are also grateful to the many students around the state who shared their informed insights.

> Elena Ermolaeva and Jessica Ross
> Huntington, West Virginia
> May, 2010

Notes

1. Movie "Michael Clayton" Warner Bros., 2008; Merton, Robert. "The Unanticipated Consequences of Purposive Social Action", *American Sociological Review*, Vol. 1, December, 1936, pp.894-904.; Colebrook, Claire. *Irony in the Work of Philosophy* (University of Nebraska Press, 2002); Healy, Tim. *The Unanticipated Consequences of Technology* Marrkkula Center for Applied Ethics, CA., 2007 http://www.scu.edu/ethics/publications/submitted/healy/consequences.html (accessed October 2, 2007).

Chapter 1

Classical Giants on Consequences of Human Actions

Robert K. Merton starts his article, "The Unanticipated Consequences of Purposive Social Action," (1936) with a statement that "in some one of its numerous forms, the problem of the unanticipated consequences of purposive action has been treated by virtually every substantial contributor to the long theory of social thought." He mentions some, without elaboration, suggesting "their contributions are by no means of equal importance." Individual contributions to the topic are briefly sketched here, in the order the thinkers were mentioned by Merton.

1.1 Niccolo Machiavelli (1469-1527)

Niccolo Machiavelli was a celebrated Florentine statesman and author of *Il Principe* whose name has long been used as an epithet or synonym for an unscrupulous politician. Political cunning and overreaching by diplomacy and intrigue came to be known as Machiavellianism. The general trend of his treatise, *Il Principe (The Prince)* (1513), is to show that rulers may resort to any treachery and artifice to uphold their arbitrary power, and whatever dishonorable acts princes may indulge in are fully set off by the insubordination of their subjects.

Machiavelli's writing related to unintended consequences is found primarily in his work *Discorsi (The Discourses)* and is related to how governments should handle unforeseen problems by turning them into positive rather than negative consequences. In some ways contrary to some of the ideals he focuses on in *The Prince*, this work proposes that disunion and unforeseen problems can be used to make positive reforms or learn from missteps of government.

Machiavelli argues that by effectively responding to unforeseen issues, or accidenti as they are called in *The Discourses*, leaders can create positive consequences rather than letting the accidenti result in a chain of negative reactions ultimately leading to negative consequences. By not characterizing accidenti as necessarily positive or negative, Machiavelli used the term only to refer to unexpected situations. It could be used to refer to a fire or flood just as easily as the liberation of a group of people from a particular regime. In *The Discourses*, Machiavelli points to numerous historical examples of accidenti and proposes solutions that make use of the accidenti to attain positive changes in society rather than letting them negatively affect it. He also stresses the importance of assuming accidenti will happen in the future and preparing to handle them as efficiently as possible. They not only have to have regard for present troubles but also

> future ones, and they have to avoid these with all their industry because, when one foresees from afar, one can easily find a remedy for them but when you wait until they come close to you the medicine is not in time because the disease has become incurable.

However Machiavelli also realized that accidenti are, by nature, unforeseen. When such occasions arise, he suggests that they be studied thoroughly so that the best possible consequences will result from them.

Machiavelli also acknowledges that not all negative accidenti can truly be remedied. In this case, he proposes that they must serve as a lesson to prevent future unfortunate consequences. Laws can be created after the fact, for instance, to keep the same accidenti from recurring. Timeliness is also crucial in Machiavelli's view because if a situation is dealt with quickly and efficiently, it prevents a downward spiral into much more negative consequences. If a negative accidenti is seen as merely that and left alone, many more unforeseen problems can stem from it, making it much more difficult to solve the original difficulty.

Machiavelli relates the issue of accidenti and eventual consequences to how a government should be formed to best deal with accidenti, mainly endorsing a "mixed regime," where not only one man or one group is in power. Using this logic, varying viewpoints are able to conquer an accidenti in different ways and the accidenti should eventually lead in a reformed, improved society. While he values a stable nation, he notes that instability creates a necessity for important reforms. He also notes that varying viewpoints within a governing body may lead to accidenti and even discord, which could lead to positive reforms as well. Machiavelli's view proposes that if a nation has some disunion at home and abroad (through dealing with other nations), more accidenti, and therefore more reforms, are possible. While a mixed regime is most favorable to Machiavelli, he also notes that by preparing laws under which a dictator could rule would provide for any possible unforeseen circumstances and should not be completely ruled out as an option.

Machiavelli's *The Discourses* is an important reference in the study of unintended consequences and how to prepare for and react to them. While his work focuses on political policy, its facets can relate to most any unforeseen consequence. By emphasizing the importance not only of how to react to unforeseen consequences but how to prepare for them, he outlines important cardinal rules for politicians and others when making important decisions. While he acknowledges that not all *accidenti* are able to be planned for in advance, he proves that, if only useful as learning tools, they can be transformed into positive consequences.[1]

Major Works
Machiavelli, Niccolo. *Il Principe (The Prince)*. Florence. 1513.
Machiavelli, Niccolo. *La Mandrangola (The Mandrake)*. Comedy. Florence. 1524.
Machiavelli, Niccolo. *Discorsi (The Discourses)*. Florence. 1531.

1.2 Giambattista Vico (1668-1744)

Giambattista Vico, the resident of Naples, went relatively unknown during his lifetime, but his studies of various social sciences gained recognition in the nineteenth century. Vico's contribution to the study of latent consequences of human action is made up of a series of ideas determining how actions are formed from human need and environment. He was particularly concerned with motivations for action that come from a primal instinct and the broader social contexts within which these instincts and actions play integral roles.

Vico used the term *sensus communis* to describe a universally shared judgment that is merely an automatic response to particular circumstances. Vico claims that these judgments, made without consideration, are simply practical responses ingrained in all human minds. He says that a judgment is not necessarily made by choice, but not by accident either. According to Vico, responses are created by a variety of circumstances surrounding an issue. All of these circumstances prescribe a context within which a judgment must be made. Each action and reaction helps to determine the next action or reaction, and often not through analysis of the situation itself but out of human drive for a particular goal.

Vico referred to the judgments as *divine*, but not in a deistic sense. He explains that *divine* providence is actually present within individuals and their surroundings. He also claims that this providence holds within itself specifications for further actions which are related to the initial action through development, regression, and evolution. The divinity of these simple judgments comes from the fact that they are latent in the human consciousness. Logical and natural responses flow from this latent consciousness and Vico believes that they prove divine in that they work together. As human actions play into their surroundings, judgments rely on the opportunities and obstacles that are provided in a given situation. Vico relates our surrounding reality to a living entity, which interacts with all circumstances, changing and elaborating them.

Essentially, Vico theorizes that many of these human actions are completely free from prior cognition, and relate more to practical needs and innate desires or feelings. Vico describes two different types of knowledge: philology and philosophy. Philology focuses on the role of human cognition in decision-making, whereas philosophy concentrates on the universal judgments of all (sensus communis). He suggest that the way to comprehensive knowledge is through the examination of both types of knowledge, concentrating on that which is commonly true as well as individually determined

According to Vico, the world operates in accordance with a system of causes and effects. Two types of wisdom—poetic and philosophical—are constantly rotating in and out of dominance. Poetic wisdom, he says, bases judgments solely on feelings, ignorant of causal relationships and other circumstances. Philosophical wisdom, however, focuses on logical reflection and analysis. The continuing cycle between feelings without judgment and cognition, he claims, originates out of necessity. He draws on these ideas to form the opinion that civilization progresses and digresses through a natural course of events that are a result of the shared judgments of all civilizations throughout history. As a society progresses towards perfection, it is always interrupted by a restoration of primal, instinctive feelings.

In critiquing Vico, it has been noted that the idea of universal human judgment (or sensus communis) neglects vast cultural, geographical, and generation differences. While there are some instincts that are present in everyone (Vico points to the fear of thunder), society does not react communally. Individual circumstances as well as those in one's environment, determine action. Whether or not comprehensive thought is given to an idea before it is acted upon, each individual instinctively may react in a completely different way. The distinction between decisions and spontaneous actions or reactions should be made in order to show that decisions are made through some sort of cognitive process, whereas immediate actions or reactions are not. While many processes of society may be completed due to latent provisions, these provisions should not necessarily be labeled as communal. The action of an individual depends on that particular individual who, while s/he might be prone to act similarly to others, is able to form judgments based on personal choices of instincts and cannot be assumed to be acting only in a way predetermined for them.[2]

Major Works
Vico, Giambattista. *Principi Di Una Scienza Nuova D'intorno Alla Comune Natura Delle Nazioni (Principles of a New Science of the Common Nature of Nations)*. Leningrad, 1940 (Orig. Pub. 1725).

1.3 Adam Smith (1723-1790)

Adam Smith, a Scottish philosopher commonly referred to as the Father of Economics, wrote "An Inquiry Into the Nature and Causes of the Wealth of Nations" in 1776. This, his most famous work, contained his well-known theory—that of the "invisible hand". Although Smith ironically only uses this phrase once in his writing, he discusses his theory at length. The "Invisible hand" theory is still discussed and argued today, particularly in the fields of economics and sociology. The most basic explanation of Smith's theory comes directly from his own words.

> Every individual necessarily labours to render the annual revenue of the society as great as he can. He generally, indeed, neither intends to promote the public interest, nor knows how much he is promoting it . . . by directing that industry in such a manner as its produce may be of the greatest value, he intends only his own gain, and he is in this, as in many other cases, led by an invisible hand to promote an end which was no part of his intention.

Smith's ideas translate into a commendation of a free market and the desire for personal advancement. His mindset was deeply rooted in his ideas of Christian values and the experience of a heavily controlled society. Smith knew that structured society was a necessary factor in the success of the "invisible hand" method and much if its efficacy depends on the desire for wealth. According to Smith, God created humans to pursue happiness—and even though they may already be happy—to seek financial gain to become happier. Once everyone is trying to achieve more and more wealth, division of labor would thrive through the hard work of each individual to become personally wealthy. Through personal attempts at financial gain, therefore, each individual would be adding to the happiness of the community, each member of which would attempt to gain the same wealth for themselves—once again leading to happiness.

Smith's contribution to the study of unintended consequences is a simple observation about human tendency. Because people are inclined to desire wealth, they unknowingly often contribute to the happiness of others by providing them with the services that they want or need. Through supply and demand, the public is able to make their desires known and the producers are able to provide them with adequate products/services.

Another of Smith's observations stated that the best way to reach a desired outcome from another individual is to offer them what they want. Because each individual is out for their own profit, all offers must seem profitable for both parties and often are. One criticism of this statement, when it is adapted on a societal rather than individual scale, is that no one person or group is able to speak for society regarding what is good, profitable, or advantageous for that particular society. The clichés of "the public good" and "the will of the people" are broad terms, assuming that one moral or value is applicable to an entire group of people, which undoubtedly have differing morals and values. This criticism of Smith's theory is known as Arrow's Impossibility Theorem, which is commonly used in reference to election results, proposing that the will of the people is often not easily determined purely by counting individual votes for each of two candidates.

Perhaps because of Smith's firm Christian beliefs, or his emphatic praise of monetary wealth, his theories seem to lump all members of society into a particular value system. For instance, Smith believed that a lucrative profession meant that a particular job was more valuable to a society than others that yield less profit. The value of one's work to another, however, is altered according to what products/services that particular person her/himself esteems, not those esteemed by their community.

As Smith realized, for the "invisible hand" to work efficiently, it must be at work in a specific kind of society. A strictly supervised society of producers and consumers with parallel value systems, all seeking the most income and the least expense through legal means is necessary. Because of human nature and the desire for "easy money" as well as the corruptive nature of economic prosperity, the seeking of maximized profits does not necessarily coincide with the benefit of society through fair prices and a semi-parallel division of labor.

Undoubtedly, Smith's discoveries have made a significant contribution to the study of economics and humanity and laid the foundation for centuries of study. His particular focus regarding the unintended consequences of human actions is positive. Through ignorance and the agenda-setting nature of personal values, one individual can benefit one or many individuals while actually only intending to benefit her/himself. Smith's theory, although it arguably neglects many environmental/societal factors, is in a broad context quite viable. Smith's observations of the happiness of a financially prosperous society center on a free market and division of labor achieved through each society member's personal quest for wealth.[3]

Major Works
Smith, Adam. *An Inquiry Into the Nature and Causes of the Wealth of Nations.* Ed. Roy H. Campbell and Andrew S. Skinner. Oxford, England: Clarendon, 1976 (Orig. Pub. 1776).

1.4 Wilhelm Wundt (1832-1920)
Wilhelm Maximilian Wundt, German physiologist and psychologist, was the first person in history to be named a "psychologist." His studies focused primarily on the mind and its workings and much of his experimentation was done through introspection, which failed to prove scientifically reliable. He is credited with the inception of the structuralism paradigm and his work, while widely ignored during his lifetime, is vast and influential.

Wundt's contributions to the theory of unintended consequences are not explicitly written as such, but provide a psychological viewpoint from which to examine the causes and effects of human actions. According to Wundt, attention is the acute awareness of one particular part of one's conscious mind. Whatever particular issue gains attention, creates an immediate and intense reaction. He studied a number of subjects to gain information about attention span in regards to exposure to stimuli focusing on a particular part of one's consciousness. In regards to latent consequences, this theory of attention may serve to partially explain the neglecting of external circumstances when reacting to stimulation from one particular part of the mind. This is applicable when studying examples of unintended consequences caused by a sense of urgency or dedication to a particular matter at hand.

Wundt also explained that the mind has various components, but in itself is also a process. Our consciousness describes the combination of components of the mind and the process through which they develop and affect changes and reactions. Sensations, ideas, feelings, volitions, and apperceptions are named as immediate experiences of the mind which lead to actions through interaction with one another. Apperception refers to the cognition of all conscious content, in other words the sum of one's experiences, emotions, feelings, and choices. Apperceptions lead to reactions. These actions are part of the volition process, where all other components of the mind lead to a chosen (or immediate) action or reaction. These processes, referred to as creative synthesis, are the development of an action from the original sensation or feeling that produces an idea to the end result, an action .

This precisely psychological description of the analytic process sheds light on all its components from a instinctual as well as cognitive point of view. Wundt outlines a process through which human action is initiated through simple feelings and other mental functions. While his theories are less focused on social ideas than experimental science, they provide important insight. Whereas most research on latent consequences is focused on what altered the goal of an action into a completely different result, his research shows the action from its birth—as an emotion or feeling. This is particularly helpful when considering human actions which are initiated to serve a particular purpose which has been deemed important based on immediate consciousness of emotional reactions. Volition resulting from these feelings and sensations is the action from which unintended ramifications often spring.[4]

Major Works
Wundt,Wilhelm. *Lectures on Human and Animal Psychology* . 1863.
Wundt,Wilhelm. *Folk Psychology.* 10 volumes. 1900-1920.

1.5 Vilfredo Pareto (1848-1923)
Italian economist Vilfredo Pareto not only made important contributions to the field of economics, but to the social sciences as well. His most noteworthy of these contributions is his concept of motivation of human action. Pareto, noticing that individuals rarely actualized the predictions of economists, looked

deeper into why people make the decisions that they make. His ideas, therefore, are applicable to the study of consequences. Because various causes for action produce varied results, his explanation of motivations lends some credit to the idea that latent consequences are frequent and often are unanticipated, because the reason an action is performed often neglects analysis of its possible consequences.

Pareto speculated that humans are not motivated necessarily by logical thought, as most economists of the time had assumed, but by sentiment. This theory was put forward in a number of his works, but most comprehensively in his *Treatise on General Sociology*. Pareto broke human actions down into two parts, *residues* and *derivations*. Residues, Pareto said, were basic human sentiments. They are, according to him, the true reason behind any human action. He believed that these reasons were not logical, but represented what a personal *felt* would benefit the most—what they truly wanted to result from a particular action. He extensively studied residues, categorizing them into six different classes. The exact functions of each class are not perhaps as important to note as the fact that they all act in conjunction with one another. Each class is represented at any given time in human history, with each dominating events at one time or another. He saw these residues as necessary and complementary to each other, creating a sort of structural functionalism in society

The derivations that Pareto refers to in his writing are essentially the validations that are given to support actions afterwards. Because actions are driven by human sentiments, rather than logical analysis, humans must create rationalizations for these actions to prove that they were, in fact, performed to achieve a particular logical purpose. Pareto also categorized derivations into four different categories: derivations of assertion, derivations of authority, derivations that are in agreement with common sentiments and principles, and derivations of verbal proof. Each of these derivations is intended to influence others to agree with an action, based on not its original intent but a cause manufactured after the action has been completed. Because it is difficult to defend a residue, or non-logical sentiment, it is easier to create a derivation to make the result of an action seem intended, rather than what it truly is—a latent consequence of a residue.

Each residue carries latent consequences, some positive and some negative. Because humans are unable to predict the exact outcome of an action, these latent consequences become manifest and sometimes require explanation. Particularly if latent consequences are negative, the original intent of an action is examined. If this intent was not logical, reasonable, analyzed, or otherwise well-formed, pressure will fall on the actor. Why were all the possible consequences not examined? Why was the most plausible avenue not taken to achieve the goal? If the original goal is changed (through derivation), perhaps this goal has been now "achieved." Even if not, the intent may simply seem more noble.

Pareto makes the case that humans do not act out of logical thought. Because most people are driven by a force inside themselves—a residue—that is often less-than-defendable, derivations are necessary to mask the residue. If logical intents are present, an action is usually far more likely to be successful. If possible consequences are examined and analyzed, negative and latent once may easily be prevented. When an action is performed on a "whim," or based solely on a personal wish, consequences may undoubtedly arise that have not been examined or expected.[5]

Major Works
Pareto, Vilfredo. *Manual on Political Economy*. New York: A. M. Kelly, 1971 (Orig. Pub. 1906 and 1909).
Pareto, Vilfredo. *Treatise on General Sociology*. New York: Harcourt, Brace, 1935 (Orig. Pub. 1916).
Pareto, Vilfredo. *The Rise and Fall of Elites*. Totowa, N.J.: Bedminster Press, 1968 (Orig. Pub.1901).

1.6 Max Weber (1864-1920)

Max Weber, prominent German sociologist and economist, was not the first scholar to explore the concept of unintended consequences; but his contribution to the topic cannot be overlooked. Weber's work *The Protestant Ethic and the Spirit of Capitalism*, published in 1904, is still discussed and debated today. The work, Weber's most acknowledged, attempts to draw a direct connection between the success of Western capitalism and Protestant values, predominantly that of work ethic.

According to Weber, Martin Luther's teaching of Berufing (or calling, in reference to duty), encouraged Protestants to work hard and dedicate themselves to their jobs. Supplementary to this value of Protestant life was that of modesty and economy, which consequently kept the Protestants from benefiting materially from their employment. Catholics, conversely according to Weber, were much more forgiving of sins including acquiring luxurious belongings. The Catholic Church, he said, was also based on a system of hierarchy with the possibility for promotion. Protestant men were focused on achieving the most they could achieve doing generally difficult work for low pay, while the Catholic men were just holding positions until a better one came along, being significantly less productive.

Because of the opportunity for upward mobility in the Catholic Church and its more relaxed attitudes towards consumption, one might imagine that Weber was pointing to the Catholic Church as the great instigator of capitalism. Instead, Weber says, the Protestant maxim of "earn and save" is what gave rise to the capitalist economy that America adopted.

His theory focused on the accumulation of wealth, not merely consumption. .As Robert Merton notes in *The Unanticipated Consequences of Purposive Social Action* (1936), Weber's ideas make the case for unanticipated actions based on basic values. The values of the Protestants were their only motivation, seemingly, for accumulating so much wealth. The irony, and unpremeditated result of their efforts to be pious, is that instead of living lives devoid of wealth or possession, they became extremely wealthy through hard work and savings.

Weber's work has come under fire for many reasons, and has been discredited by a number of scholars. One reason for this is that, according to Lloyd, capitalism had existed in one form or another long before Protestantism. Another criticism of his theory was its religious nature, which eventually led to the adaptation of the idea of religious obligation to professional dedication.

Weber's argument seems to be based on the idea of tolerance of a particularly undesired consequence (excessive capital gain). This tolerance, according to Weber, then eventually made way for the emergence of a powerful capitalist economy. By justifying acquisition of capital in a community where it was previously avoided, the strong working morals of this group are the same morals that essentially expunged their other convictions. By allowing for this shift in attitude, the Protestants unintentionally gave up one of their own principles and perhaps unknowingly thrust themselves into a capitalist economy that might have previously been deemed impious. As Weber says, it is the seeking out of wealth that has eventually removed the responsibility (religious or otherwise) factor from work and transformed it into a quest for greed. "In the field of its highest development, in the United States, the pursuit of wealth, stripped of its religious and ethical meaning, tends to become associated with purely mundane passions, which often actually give it the character of sport" (Weber 1976).[6]

Major Works
Weber, Max. *Economy and Society: An Outline of Interpretive Sociology*. Trans. G. Roth and G. Wittich. New York: Bedminster, 1968 (Orig. pub. 1922)
Weber, Max. *The Protestant Ethic and the Spirit of Capitalism*. Trans. Talcott Parsons. Introduction by Anthony Giddens. New York: Scribner, 1976 (Orig. pub. 1904-1905).

1.7 Graham Wallas (1858-1932)
In Graham Wallas' writing the *Art of Thought* (1926), he organized the creative process into four distinct stages. Later, a fifth stage was added by scholars and has widely been accepted since. Wallas' contribution to the theory of latent consequences lies within these stages. Wallas considered creation and creativity evolutionary actions. Through the creative process, the human mind reasons, analyzes, and advances ideas, putting them through various stages of thought which often revert back and forth between one another rather than following a linear, chronological system.

Wallas' first stage was *preparation*. In the preparation stage, Wallas claims that the individual recognizes her/his interest in a particular topic This stage includes the individual's prior knowledge and experience regarding the topic. This stage requires very little analysis, but rather is similar to instinct.

The next stage that Wallas describes is *incubation*, through which the individual thinks deeply about the problem or idea. In this stage, the problem is made specific not through analysis or intense cognition, but through intuition and the rough development of ideas.

The third stage of creativity according to Wallas is *insight*, which he describes as "illumination." This stage occurs when the answer to the problem appears suddenly. This stage also requires no real analysis, but another example of instinct. Because these first steps, performed without much logical thought or reason, can be dangerous to act upon, Wallas developed his fourth stage.

The fourth stage of the creative process is *evaluation*. During the evaluation process, insights are analyzed and researched. He also referred to this stage as "verification." Verification refers to the legitimizing of the idea. Evaluation involves making sure that the solutions are possibly and probably attainable. This stage may lead the individual back to previous stages if the idea is determined to be faulty.

The fifth stage, not one of Wallas' own but worth mentioning, is referred to as *elaboration*. This stage highlights the importance of putting the idea into action. Through elaboration, the exact course of action is determined and its necessity is verified.

One complaint about Wallas' stages is that his theories are purely cognitive and that he backs them up with no science or evidence of any kind. The stages are also seen as overly structured, not allowing much passage back and forth between different forms of creativity. While there are some faults with Wallas' ideas, his stages lay out a basic guideline for the development of ideas and the actions that follow them. Wallas, an English economist and teacher, places value on the analytic side of decision-making, focusing on various ways of legitimizing an idea and determining the possible outcomes of the proposed action. His stages create a general example for a process through which actions could carry with them a minimum of negative unanticipated or unintended consequences.[7]

Major Works
Wallas, Graham. *The Great Society: A Psychological Analysis*. New York: Macmillan Co , 1914.
Wallas, Graham. *The Art of Thoughts*. New York: Harcourt, Brace and Company, 1926.

Notes

1. See: Benet, William Rose, ed. *The Reader's Encyclopedia. An Encyclopedia of World Literature and the Arts*. (New York: Thomas Y.Crowell Company, 1948); McCormick, John P. "Addressing the Political Exception: Machiavelli's "Accidents' and the Mixed Regime." *American Political Science Review*. (Cambridge University Press, 1993).
2. "Giambattista Vico". *Stanford Encyclopedia of Philosophy* Stanford University, 11 June 2003. http://plato.stanford.edu/entries/vico/ (accessed March 1, 2008); Shotter, John. *Vico, Wittgenstein, and Bakhtin: 'Practical Trust' in Dialogical Communities*. University of New Hampshire, November 9, 1996.http://www.massey.ac.nz/~alock/virtual

/js.htm, (accessed March 1, 2008).

3. Joyce, Helen. *Adam Smith and the Invisible Hand*. Plus Mar. 2001. http://plus.maths.org/issue14/features/smith (accessed February 1, 2008); Schenk, Robert E. *Unintended Consequences*. Cybereconomics. St. Joseph's College, 2007 http://ingrimayne.com/econ/Introduction/Unintend.html (accessed February 1, 2008).

4. Watson, R.I. Sr. *Wilhelm Wundt*. The Great Psychologists. 4th ed. (New York: Lippincott Co. 1978).

5. Thornton, James. *A Concise Overview of His Life, Works, and Philosophy*. 1997 http://jkalb.freeshell.org/misc/pareto.html (accessed February 11, 2008); *Vilfredo Pareto*. New School University Profiles. New School University http://cepa.newschool.edu/het/profiles/pareto.htm (accessed February 11, 2008).

6. Max Weber. New School University, February 14, 2003 http://cepa.newschool.edu/het/profiles/weber.htm (accessed January 18, 2008); Lloyd, David F. Max Weber: A Compulsion for Work. *Vision*, October 2004 http://www.vision.org/visionmedia/printerfriendly.aspx?id=536#Top (accessed January 18, 2008).; Merton, Robert K. "The Unanticipated Consequences of Purposive Social Action" *American Sociological Review* 1 (December 1936): 894-904; Weber, Max. *The Protestant Ethic and the Spirit of Capitalism*. Trans. Talcott Parsons. Introduction by Anthony Giddens. (New York: Scribner, 1976 (Orig. pub. 1904-1905)).

7. Hills, Gerald E. *Opportunity Recognition as a Creative Process* Babson.edu Babson University, March 2000 http://www.babson.edu/entrep/fer/papers99/X/X_A/X_A.html (accessed March 1, 2008).

Chapter 2

Gender and Family

2.1 History of Family law

2.1.1 John Milton, England, 1643

The history of family law is a fertile area for unforeseen consequences. As early as in the seventeenth century, John Milton in England set out to bring Anglican Church doctrine into line with that of the Continental Protestant Church. Indeed, he went even further than they, actually laying the groundwork for what would one day be a widely recognized justification for dissolving marriages: he argued, first, that incompatibility was by itself a proper ground for divorce; and second, that divorce should be a "private matter." The first of Milton's four essays on divorce was published in 1643, just after Parliament had passed a resolution asking the governing body of the Anglican Church to revise various aspects of ecclesiastical law. Although Milton aimed to influence the Church to moderate its divorce posture, the radical character of his proposals had precisely the opposite effect. The conservative divines of the Westminster Assembly reacted very negatively to the ideas set forth in his essays and pulled back from whatever inclinations they had had to "Europeanize" English divorce laws.[1]

2.1.2 No-Fault Divorce Law, USA, 1970

Divorce has accompanied the institution of marriage for centuries. Divorce originated in Ancient Mesopotamia where the Mesopotanian people were allowed to divorce freely. However, before the divorce could be finalized, the reasons for the separation had to be reviewed and declared adequate. Divorce has been prevalent in many other cultures throughout history, for example, the Romans believed in "matrimonia debent esse libera," which meant marriage ought to be free.

Divorce in the United States today is defined as, "the dissolution of a marriage contracted between a man and woman, by the judgment of a court of competent jurisdiction, or by an act of the legislature." Currently in the United States, there are multiple types of divorce including: at-fault, summary, uncontested, collaborative, mediated, and no-fault.

The two prime intentions behind the creation of the no-fault divorce law were, first, to help those needing to escape intolerable marriages, especially abused wives, without any evidence against the other spouse and to protect children from bitter court battles; the second resulted from judges and lawyers wanted to remove false incriminations from the divorce process.

Before the no-fault law became established, married couples were required to complete a multi-step program in order to absolve the marriage. This process mandated one party would have to accuse the other of serious fault such as adultery, abuse, or abandonment. Following the first accusation, the second party would generally make similar accusations in order to defend themselves. Lastly, the case would be presented to a judge where he or she would make the final decision of whether the divorce would be granted.

Due to these prerequisites, many couples were forced to lie and engage in collusive adultery or claim cruelty against one spouse. An example of collusive adultery is when a married man or woman would conspire to have his or her spouse arrive home and discover him or her in an adulterous situation. This then allowed one person in the relationship to claim adultery and move forward with a divorce. This tactic was so common that lawyers frequently advised collusive adultery to couples who wanted out of a marriage. Even more frequent than collusive adultery was the accusation of cruelty. This accusation became the popular, generic reason for divorce presented to many judges. Statistics show that around 1950, prior to the no-fault law, seventy percent of San Francisco's divorce cases were filed upon some grounds of cruelty.

Also, prior to the no-fault divorce law, the cost of a divorce, for the attorney alone ranged from ten thousand to fifty thousand dollars. This did not include other expenses such as hiring investigators, moving expenses, or child support.

Oklahoma was the first state to pass the no-fault divorce law in 1953, however it was not frequently utilized. The law finally became popular seventeen years later when California signed the law into the Family Law Act of 1970. The Act was signed by Governor Ronald Regan. The Act was the first in our nation to abolish the concept of fault in divorce proceedings and replacing the old system with the sole possible reasoning of irreconcilable differences. At the same time, the Act removed evidence of marital misconduct from consideration of financial settlements. Under the new Act, the courts were required to divide community property equally and to award support on the basis of financial need and ability to pay. Now, we come to a list of consequences of this new law.

First, the law has increased the ease at which a divorce may be obtained, thus, increasing the rate of divorce. The divorce rate increased drastically from

1960 to 1980—from nine in one thousand people successfully completing a divorce to twenty-three in one thousand people. Today, the divorce rate is at a shocking fifty percent, meaning one in every two marriages ends in divorce. Those against the law claim that over eighty percent of divorces are one sided. This means that one person from the union does not desire a divorce and the other partner is free to leave without reason, abandoning their promise of marriage and support. Absent fathers is another unanticipated consequence of no-fault divorce law, emerging more and more frequently. According to a study cited in *Fortune Magazine,* while many men expressed the desire for custody of their children during a divorce, only 13% ever formally requested it. The study also indicated that children often had little or no contact with their fathers after the divorce. This points to the possibility that some husbands may be leaving their families to escape the responsibility—or perhaps feelings of regret or inadequacy. They may also just be looking for another woman, and have no desire to remain in contact with their previous family. Also stated in the study, divorced men find it much easier to remarry than do divorced women. They also usually have greater ease earning enough money to support themselves alone.

The discussion of the second consequence should be preceded with a reminder of a problem of causal imputation—to what extent particular consequence ought to be attributed to particular actions since consequences can have a number of causes. It is possible that the no-fault divorce law with the equal division of assets has caused men and women to hesitate before entering into marriage, ultimately choosing not to marry to prevent losing personal possessions and property. The births rates to unmarried women jumped from eleven percent to thirty-three percent. Nationally, 1.3 million kids were born out-of-wedlock each year since 1970. Statistics also show that following the no-fault law, the United States experienced the highest rates of teen sexual activity, teen pregnancy, births to teenage mothers, and out of wedlock births.

Supporters of the law insist on positive consequences of the law. They cite statistics that demonstrate states with the no-fault law have seen a decline in the rates of domestic violence. They also claim that there is less conflict involved in the divorce process which inputs less stress on the children possibly drawn into the situation. They suggest that it has helped to reduce the caseloads in family courts and made financial settlement decisions based on need and ability to pay rather than on fault.

The opponents of the law argue that a dependent's living standards are lowered and many women find themselves suddenly alone, and with less assistance than they would have received through old divorce laws. Previous divorce regulations provided for the compensation of the party deemed not responsible for the failure of the marriage, commonly the wife. No-fault divorce laws have implemented a policy of equal appropriation of property between ex-spouses. This is done under the assumption that it creates equality. Unfortunately, recently divorced couples rarely have equal financial assets, job security or prospects, and ability to be self-supporting. A woman who has gained custody of her children in a divorce, consequently, would receive the same amount of money as her single former husband. According to Hacker in *Fortune Magazine*, only 15% of divorced women currently receive alimony. They are also now less likely to receive child support. Even if they are rewarded child support, enforcement is not strict and payments are often not made. When payments are received, they cover only one half of the cost of care for each child. Claire Renzetti cites a 1999 study which concluded that divorced women's standard of living decreased by 36%. The decrease was only 18% for men. Although this trend is changing, as noted earlier, the disadvantage that men experience after a divorce between two providers is significantly less than that of a woman.

Complicating the issue, many women (particularly older women) have spent their married lives working at home while their husbands have provided the primary income. Although this trend is changing with most families having two working adults, women who have not needed to have jobs for years, even decades, are forced to find a way into the workforce. Commonly they have few marketable skills and are unable to find work that pays well, if they are able to find it at all. With the added responsibility of single-parenthood, working may also be difficult.

Another disadvantage for divorced women stems from the welfare reform of 1996 (The Personal Responsibility and Work Opportunity Reconciliation Act). According to the law's provisions, women and children impoverished by divorce are eligible only for temporary and limited assistance, if they are eligible for any assistance at all. They are also forced quickly into finding a job, and balancing it with parental responsibilities. These benefits, if provided, are commonly not a sufficient means of assistance.

It has been suggested that no-fault divorce laws significantly contribute to the feminization of poverty. This new culture of single mothers, many times thrust suddenly into poverty, is growing at a surprising rate. The economic disadvantages of women after divorce are an unanticipated and unfortunate consequence of a law with good intentions. While no-fault divorce laws have spared many families the pain of bitter court trials, a new pain has arisen in the form of female and child poverty. Inefficient assistance for the victims of these situations increases the seriousness of the problem. A more critical look at these outside circumstances may have prevented the failure of no-fault divorce laws to fully achieve their purpose. As a California lawyer said later of her support for no-fault divorce laws: "I assumed, in the optimistic spirit of the reformers, that ... no-fault divorce could only have positive result."[2]

2.2 Genocide in Rwanda on Women in Parliament, 1994

In Rwanda the genocide led by the Hutu Army and militias nearly wiped out the male Tutsi population. When the killing ended in July 1994 women outnumbered men by seven to three. The government recognized a shortage of men, and set aside nearly a third of parliamentary seats for female representatives.

Now women make up half of Parliament—the largest percentage anywhere in the world. The revolution for women has come about partly by necessity.[3]

2.3 Demographic Change in Japan on Women in Education, 2003—

In earlier decades of the twentieth century, higher education for Japanese women served to prepare them for their traditional gender roles—that of a devoted wife and mother. Japanese society also upholds a very clear division of labor with the home, and being a homemaker was, and for some still is, the highest goal women should strive to attain. Inside the home is the domain where it is acceptable for the female to take the dominant role, so it became desirable for these women to have some advanced education. After all, they will be aiding in the education process of the next generation. These mothers must pass on cultural values and wisdom to her children, so she herself must have some knowledge of this. The best way to saturate individuals with socialized norms and values of a given society is through many years in the educational system. Also, the university in Japan is an excellent place to meet one's future spouse. Rather than just seeking a higher degree, the Japanese woman might also be seeking a husband. The desire for a wife with some higher education became particularly pronounced following World War II. However, in line with gender roles, the husband was certainly expected to have a better education than his wife or potential wife. In turn, Japanese parents both did not wish to put forth two much money on a daughter's education and did not wish to overeducate her fro fear that it might ruin her marriage prospects.

The educational system in Japan as a whole indicated the prevalence of gender inequality within the system. The higher education system in Japan is a two-tired system. There are two-year junior colleges and traditional four-year colleges. There are both private and public universities. Unlike in the United States, a four-year private university in Japan is less prestigious than any four-year public university. Of course, any junior college degree is less prestigious than any four-year university degree. Lesser still are the technological colleges which train students for industrial careers. Even below these are the specialized training colleges, where the male to female ratio is considerably more balanced than in better institutions.

The ratios of male to female enrollment in these different institutions reveal a great deal of gender inequality within this system. The most clear cut difference, particularly following the WWII era, is the saturation of women in the junior college system. The large number of junior colleges were formed as a solution to the problem of a desire for women to obtain a higher education without becoming overly education and without too much expenditure of financial resource. Thus, women flooded the junior college system. In 1985, women comprised almost 90 percent of the student body of junior colleges.

The recent years show the increase in the enrollment rates of women in four-year universities. Why? Mainly, it is due to a demographic switch. Like any industrialized nation Japan experiences a drop in birth rates which is now closer to only one child per family rather than the previous two or three children per family. In turn, there are simply far fewer young people of the college age. Thus, where students once had to compete among themselves to gain admission into Japanese universities, the universities must now compete over the low numbers of potential students. Women began to look more and more attractive to the college admission boards. Furthermore, with fewer children in each family, parents have more money to put into their daughter's education, so more of them can afford to send them to a four-year university rather than a junior college. Also, given the low numbers of students, the cost of higher education has dropped somewhat. This demographic trend could eventually lead to the demise of the junior college system and a higher rate of gender equality in the Japanese higher education system.[4]

2.4 Honor Killing and Suicide, Western Europe, 2005—

In 2006, for the very first time, a court in Europe sentenced nine members of the same family for the honor killing of a female relative. Honor killings, where a woman is murdered for the shame that she is said to have brought on her family, are a growing phenomenon in Western Europe. In December 2005 Nazil Afzal, a spokesman of Britain's Crown Prosecution Service stated that the United Kingdom has had "at least a dozen honor killings" between 2004 and 2005. British police are investigating more that 100 cases of women who died under mysterious circumstances. Germany was shocked in 2005 by the murder of Hatin Surucu, a young Turkish woman who was killed by three brothers because she was "a whore who lived like a German." A German women's organization states that "There are no concrete statistics available, but unofficial estimates [of honor killings] are considered to be high. We get calls from women caught in difficult situations almost every tow weeks."

As in the Surucu case the general practice so far has been to sentence only the actual murderers. In 2006, however, a jury of the Ostre Landsret ruled that not only the man who pulled the trigger was guilty, but every family member who collaborated in "punishing" Ghazala Khan, an 18-year old Danish-born woman of Pakistani origin, who was shot by her brother, 30-year old Akhtar Abbas, on 23 September 2005, two days after her marriage.

Ghazala had married an Afghan man, 27-year old Emal Khan, against the wishes of her father. An aunt, the youngest sister of Ghazala's mother, who had told the young couple that she would try to reconcile them with her family, asked them to come to Slagelse train station. Her brother Akhtar shot her dead in front of the station and wounded Emal Khan, who survived the murder attempt.

A Danish judge sentenced Akhtar Abbas to 16 years in gaol, and the father, 57-year old Ghulam Abbas, to life imprisonment. The aunt and two uncles were given 16 years as well. Other members of the family and friends who had helped to track down Ghazala received sentences of between 8 and 16 years. The Danish verdict is historic, not only because the entire clan was punished but also because the head of the family, who ordered the killing, was given a heavier sentence than the actual murderer. Families often choose a family member who is still a minor to carry out an honor assassination because, being a minor, he is likely to get a more lenient sentence under Western law.

The Danish verdict, the similar rulings in Netherlands have the explicitly intended consequence to stop the barbaric practice but they create a latent ramification: an increase of female suicide.

The name "honor killing" is not entirely appropriate. Rather, the action is better described as shame killings. Shame is perceived to have been brought on a family and they murder to remove the shame and most recently women take their own lives.[5]

2.5 Globalization, Women's Labor Force Participation, and Feminization of Migration

Labor migrants have traditionally been men. For instance, Chinese laborers in the United States in the 1800s were overwhelmingly unmarried men. In South Africa, men have long left home to work in mines and industries. Men from South Asia and Northern Africa have traveled to the Persian Gulf to work in the oil industry. Traditionally, women were left at home to care for the children and elders and to wait for the return of their men.

Increasingly, it is women who are leaving. Wealthiest countries in the last decades have been flooded with immigrant female domestic workers. Ironically, it was the movement of women into professional positions in Europe and North America that led to the recent surge in international domestic migrants. The Latina domestic in the United States, the Turkish domestic in Germany, Filipina maids in Hong Kong, Sri Lankan's in Jordan have become commonplace. This pattern is now expanding around the globe, as pockets of prosperity become magnets for domestic workers from less-thriving economies. By almost any measure, the housemaids' salaries are tiny—some as little as 30 cents an hour, plus room and board, for 14-hour days of cooking and cleaning. Yet, these women have been able to save for new homes in their villages. And as services that used to be taken for granted now keep their families alive, the women see themselves differently.[6]

Critical Thinking Questions

For each "case study" in the Chapter:

1. Discuss the Direction of change. For example, good intentions may lead to negative consequences; or, something positive may come up as a result of negative conditions; the consequence is neither good nor bad but a modification of the previous condition, etc.

2. Discuss the Nature of consequences—unintended, unforeseen, ironic.

3. What did go "wrong" and why? Why was the outcome unforeseen/ unintended? Was it due to ignorance, error, immediate interest, basic values, intensity of the action, etc.?

4. Discuss the Nature of an action—was it unorganized or formally organized?

Notes

1. V. Mollenkott,. *Milton on divorce.* (unpublished paper, Department of English, Paterson State College, Paterson, N.J.; 1977); B. Farber,. *Introduction to Willard Waller, The old love and the new.* (Carbondale: Southern IllinoisUniversity Press; 1967); John Scanzoni, "A Historical Perspective on Husband-Wife Bargaining Power and Marital Dissolution." (pp. 20-36 in: *Divorce and Separation. Context, Causes, and Consequences*, edited by George Levinger and Oliver C. Moles, New York: Basic Books, 1979).

2. "Divorce." *Divorce.* http://www.lectlaw.com/def/d187.htm (accessed August 3, 2008); Devine, Joseph. "No-Fault Divorce History." *Ezine Articles* June 19, 2008 http://ezinearticles.com/?no-fault-divorce-history (accessed August 3, 2008); Hacker, Andrew W. "Post-Marital Economics." *Fortune Magazine* 23 Dec. 1985; "Marriage Statistics." *Chicagoland Marriage Resource Center.* http://www.chicagolandmarriage.org/marriage_statistics.htm (accessed August 3, 2008); "Divorce Support." *Divorce Support.* http://divorcesupport.about.com/od/maritalproblems/i/nofault_fault.htm (accessed August 3, 2008); Renzetti, Claire M. *Women, Men, and Society.* 5th ed. (Boston: Pearson Eduation, 2003).

3. Hammer, Joshua, "Healing Powers." *Newsweek Magazine.* April 3, 2006.

4. Raymo, James M. & Iwasawa, Miho. "Marriage Market Mismatches in Japan: Alternative View of the Relationship between Women's Education and Marriage." *American Sociological Review*, 2005, Vol. 70 Issue 5 pp. 801-822; Meguro, Yoriko, *Education for Women and Girls in Japan—Progress and Challenges.* Prepared for UNESCO Regional Seminar: Towards the Gender Equality in Basic Education. Major Challenges to Meet Dakar EFA Goals, 2001 (accessed November 11, 2006) http:://www.unescobkk.org/fileadmin/User_upload/appeal/gender/genderequalityJapan.doc; Curtin, J. Sean. "Gender Equality in Japanese Education: Part One-Male and Female Participation rates in Higher Education." *Glocom Platform Social Trends*, #42, 2003, http://www.glocom.org/special_topics/social_trends/20030617trends_s42/index.html (accessed November 11, 2006); Curtin, J. Sean. "Gender Equality in Japanese Education: Part Two-The Development of the Two-year Women's Junior College System." *Glocom Platform Social Trends*, #43, 2003 http://www.glocom.org/special_topics/social_trends/20030625_trends_s45/index.html (accessed November 11, 2006); Curtin, J. Sean. "Gender Equality in Japanese Education: Part Four- The Changing Nature of the University Prospective Student Relationship." *Glocom Platform Social Trends* #47, 2003 http://www.glocom.org/special_topics/social_trends/20030625_trends_s47/index.html (accessed November 11, 2006); Curtin, J. Sean. "Gender Equality in Japanese Education: Part Five-Gender Bias in the Parental Allocation of Financial Resources for Education." *Glocom Platform Social Trends* #48, 2003 http://www.glocom.org/special_topics/social_trends/20030625_trends_s48/index.html (accessed November 11, 2006); Nagasawa, Makoto. "Gender Stratifica-

tion in Japanese Higher Education." *International Higher Education* Number 40. 2005 http:///bc.edu/bc_org/avp/soe/cihe/newsletter/Number0/p10_Nagasawa.htm (accessed November 11, 2006).

5. Laenen, Filip van, *Danes Sentence Entire Clan for Honour Killing*, July2, 2006. (accessed October 16, 2006); Brussels Journal 2008. Kentucky Public Television, Fall.

6. Sernau, Scott, *Global Problems. The Search for Equity, Peace, and Sustainability*. Second Edition. (Pearson; Parrenas, 2009); Rhacel Salazar, *Servants of Globalization. Women, Migration, and Domestic Work*. (StanfordUniversity Press, 2002); Tolan, Sandy, *Sri Lanka: An Exodus of Women* (Radioprogram, 2003. Worlds of Difference, Homelands Productions. Transcript available online at www.homelands.org/worlds/srmaids/html.

Chapter 3

Race and Ethnicity

3.1 The Allotment Act of 1887 (the Dawes Act)

The saga of the improvement of Indian affairs *was* and *is* marked by a continuous failure because it assumed that the organizational logic of Indian peoples was the same as that of the Anglos. The overt goal of the (General) Allotment Act of 1887 was to convert Indians into small farmers. The allotment plan particularly attempted to assimilate the Indian into white civilization. According to Lyman Tyler, the trend of government Indian policy during the 1870s and the 1880s was to further minimize the functions of tribal leaders and tribal institutions and to continually strengthen the position of the government representative and his subordinates, and to improve the effectiveness of their programs to break down traditional patterns within the Indian communities. The subsequent agreement and statutes allotting tribal lands were enforced with a frightening efficiency. Even on reservations so crowded with trees one could not walk the lands or in barren desert areas, allotment was carried out in defiance of common sense because Congress had so decreed. The act subdivided the reservations and allotted tribal land to individual tribal members in 40- or 160- acre parcels, with the federal government purchasing the remaining lands of the tribe.

The act, in fact, had facilitated the passage of millions of acres of land out of Indian hands and into those of whites. By 1934 two thirds of the tribal lands had passed into white ownership; by 1940 tribes possessed only 2.3 percent of the country's land mass. With the loss of their lands, Indians had fallen into a state of rural poverty and depression.[1]

3.2 Indian Reorganization Act (IRA) of 1934

The Indian Reorganization Act (or Wheeler-Howard Act; also known as The New Deal) of 1934 was to be of considerable benefit to Indian peoples, since it made a frontal attack on many of the most vexatious problems. Land allotment was stopped. Indian tribes were encouraged to organize themselves as governments that would receive formal recognition from the federal government.

But the impact of the IRA had been deeper and greater than anticipated. According to Wax & Buchanan, initially legislators had simply wanted to relieve Indian poverty and bring monies to their depression-ridden communities. But the IRA was doing more: it was denying to local whites the opportunities to use or gain control over Indian resources, and it was giving to Indian communities more political clout. Local white groups were becoming upset by this shift in power. Also, Indians being themselves diverse and having varied, even opposed, interests, some were bound to dislike the Indian New Deal.

Wax & Buchanan (1975) analyze further the assumptions and fallacies inherent in the New Deal for native Americans. First, it was assumed that Indians would assimilate, even if at their own speed. Instead, what was to happen, was that Indians would change, but nonetheless retain a strong political and social sense of Indian identity. Second, there was the familiar assumption that Indians were essentially alike. John Collier's, a Commissioner of Indian Affairs, personal experiences had been in the Southwest with the tightly organized Pueblo peoples. His background did not prepare him to cope with diversity of Indian interests and preferences, some of which were individualistic or Anglo oriented. Third, the New Dealers assumed that Indians, if given the opportunity, would organize themselves into unified tribal government that would operate by majority rule as effective forces for tribal self-help. But most North American Indian peoples had little familiarity with the Anglo system of majority rule, instead, they operated on a different organizational logic.

Indian groups operated on the basis of consensus and without coercion. When people were troubled, they met and discussed until they agreed on what should be done; if they could not reach unanimity, they continued their discussion, as no action could be undertaken. The legislative procedures, familiar to whites and crystallized as "Roberts Rules of Order" permit a majority of an assembly to mobilize its strength and commit the group to action even in the face of minority dissent. Traditional Indians did not vote "Nay" and then accede to the will of the majority, but rather they refused to participate and their cooperation could not be enforced.[2]

3.3 Land Ownership and African American Class Divide

While the Native Americans were hurt by allotment efforts, the African American land ownership, arguably, is one of historical causes of their current class divide. After the abolishing of slavery some former slaves were able to obtain property, as a result of personal effort or due to the Southern Homestead Act.

Henry Louis Gates Jr., a professor at Harvard University, studied the family trees of 20 successful African-Americans, people in fields ranging from entertainment and sports (Oprah Winfrey, the track star Jackie Joyner-Kersee) to space travel and medicine (the astronaut Mae Jemison and Ben Carson, a pediatric neurosurgeon). He discovered an astonishing pattern: 15 of the 20 descend from one line of former slave who managed to obtain property by 1920—a time when only 25 percent of all African-American families owned property.

Ten years after slavery ended, Constantine Winfrey, Oprah's great-grandfather, bartered eight bales of cleaned cotton (4,000 pounds) that he picked on his own time for 80 acres of prime bottomland in Mississippi. Whoopi Goldberg's great-great-grandparents received their land through the Southern Homestead Act. According to Gates, there is a meaningful correlation between the success of accomplished African-Americans today and their ancestors' property ownership. In case "40 acres and a mule" had really been an official government policy in the Reconstruction South, black-white relations and class composition of African American community would be different today.

In November 2007 the Pew Research Center published the astonishing finding that 37 percent of African-Americans polled felt that "blacks today can no longer be thought of as a single race" because of a widening class divide. By a ratio of 2 to 1, the report says, blacks say that the values of poor and middle-class blacks have gone more dissimilar over the past decade.

There are affluent blacks but the most part of the African American community is below the poverty line. The median net income of non-Hispanic black household in 2004 was only $11,800; today 69 percent of black babies are born out of wedlock; and 45 percent of black households with children are headed by women.

How did this happen? There are various theories—from slavery and segregation to the decline of factory jobs, crack cocaine, drug laws and outsourcing. The historical basis of the gap between the black middle class and underclass shows that ending discrimination, by itself, would not eradicate black poverty and dysfunction. We also need intervention to promulgate a middle-class ethic of success among the poor, while expanding opportunities for economic betterment. People who own property feel a sense of ownership in their future and their society. They study, save, work, strive and vote. People trapped in a culture of tenancy do not.

The chasm between classes in the black community is partly the result of social forces set in motion by the dismal failure of "40 acres and a mule."[3]

3.4 The Jim Crow, White Violence, Civil Rights Act of 1964, and the Role of Television Coverage

The Civil Rights Movement of the 1950s and 1960s was one of the most influential movements for social change in American history. After decades of disenfranchisement at the hands of American whites—particularly in the South—

African Americans took a stand against the political, social, and economic oppression that they had endured since arriving in the United States as slaves. The Civil Rights Movement and moves towards racial equality, such as the Brown v. Board of Education verdict (1954), incited segregationists and racists in the South and led to a series of violent and nonviolent actions by those who resisted the changes that were being brought about. These actions were intended to stop integration and the advancement of blacks in America. Instead, the white aggression led to unintended consequences. Due in great part to the attention of television news broadcasts, the hostile Southerners did not stop the Civil Rights Movement. They propelled it through gradual changes in public opinion.

At the time that the Civil Rights Movement was getting under way, television was becoming an integral part of American society. In 1955, televisions could be found in 92% of American homes—up from 56% previously. Technical advances were making it possible for portable cameras to go to the scene of news stories and evening news programs had been lengthened from 15 minutes to 30 minutes. Civil rights protests and boycotts began to get national media attention, as did the responses from segregationists. Black churches were bombed and blacks or anyone associated with the Civil Rights Movement were terrorized and even murdered throughout the South. While Southern whites felt that their actions would scare blacks back into complacent oppression, these actions actually helped to garner support for the movement from people who otherwise may have been oblivious or apathetic to the struggle.

Because news about African Americans was largely ignored at the time unless it involved black-on-white crime, the leaders of the Civil Rights Movement knew that the presence of whites at their events would bring even more media attention. The deaths of white civil rights workers Andrew Goodman and Michael Schwerner, and James Chaney, an African American, certainly proved this to be true. The white element caused a stir in suburban communities and brought the issue of civil rights closer to home. Known as crisis-television, the coverage of violence and tragedies during the Civil Rights Movement brought the turbulent South into American living rooms. This type of coverage continued throughout other social movements of the 1960s and is at the center of television news today.

Coverage of tragedies and the mistreatment of blacks were not only eye-catching, but led to policy changes through changes in public opinion. For instance, the use of dogs and fire hoses by Birmingham Police Commissioner Bull Connor against peaceful African American men, women, and children led to the passage on the Public Accommodations Act of 1964. Television broadcasts of violent reactions to a voting rights march in Selma, Alabama also led to policy change. The Voting Rights Act, which protected the suffrage of thousands of African Americans, was passed after demonstrators were attached with cattle prods, clubs, and whips at the hands of Sheriff Jim Clark and his men. These disgusting images were a powerful force in the advancement of the Civil Rights Movement and they certainly would have been much less effective as news stories in print.

Civil rights leader Martin Luther King, Jr. also brought attention to the movement, using eloquent speeches with positive messages to counter the brutal violence of white segregationists. These speeches became the loudest voice for the movement and elicited emotional responses from blacks and whites alike. Journalist Jack Nelson, who has been reporting for over 50 years, says that Dr. King would often arrive late for televised events. "But," he says, "there was one thing we could count on: he would never arrive so late that waiting television crews could not get their coverage of what he did or said onto the networks' evening news programs." The mass media—and television in particular—was a strategic tool in stopping black oppression.

News producers and civil rights leaders alike realized how useful sensational images of violent responses to peaceful protests were. News producers saw ratings and civil rights leaders saw the opportunity to spread their message. Despite the fact that blacks rarely were given the chance to speak directly to the cameras to tell their stories, the stories were told through intense images that shocked much of the nation. This shock gradually led to a change in the way that many Americans saw racial issues at the time. Without necessarily taking either side on the issue, television news programs showed Americans the images of the Civil Rights Movement. These images, in turn, showed how peaceful and positive the movement was in the face of such brutal backlash from segregationists and Jim Crow proponents.

By countering peaceful demonstrations by Civil Rights leaders and volunteers, white segregationists in the South felt that they were hindering the advancement of people that they felt were not entitled to equal treatment under the law. Unintended consequences, however, came about due to the violence and intensity of their reactions. At the time the fight for civil rights was taking form in America, the television was becoming an invaluable part of society. Enthralling and gut-wrenching images of white-on-black violence in the South did not garner public support for segregationist policy. In fact, it caused public outcry against it. By using unnecessarily violent means to reach their end, segregationists failed to reach it. With the aid of media attention, public opinion and government policy gradually took the side of the Civil Rights Movement over that of Jim Crow "justice."[4]

3.5 Outsourcing Affirmative Action

What's more important—making sure students can attend good schools, or making sure schools are diverse? Can school districts consider race as a way to keep classrooms diverse?

Affirmative action was first coined in 1961 by President Kennedy, who created the Committee for Economic Opportunity. His executive order mandated that projects using federal funds use "affirmative action" to ensure hiring practices were free of racial bias.

As the civil rights movement swelled, affirmative action was further defined by President Johnson in a 1963 speech at Howard University: "You do not take a man hobbled for years by chains, liberate him and bring him to the starting race, saying, "You are free to compete with all others." Today, after several court challenges, race alone—rather than social disparity—has become a more relevant factor in university admissions, according to the American Association of Affirmative Action.

"Affirmative action is no longer a compensation for past discriminations," said Shirley Wilcher, the Association's executive director. "Today it is divorced from overcoming disadvantage." Many universities brag about diversity but their admission policies increasingly reflect race and social class, rather than economic need. Now, 46 years after the term "affirmative action" was first coined, efforts to help the economically disadvantaged are shifting as American universities cater to an "elite class" of socially successful blacks.

In 2003, the Supreme Court ruled in favor of affirmative action in a case brought against the Michigan Law School. But in another suit against the undergraduate school, the courts ruled against a system that gave preferential points, but allowed the college could take race into account in admission.

Wilcher graduated from one of the all-female Seven Sisters colleges in 1973 and recently returned to her alma matter for a black alumni conference and discovered there were fewer African-Americans than foreign nationals—a marked difference from her day. "We had a discussion because there were so many native-born Caribbeans and Africans, and it created a lot of tension among students," said Wilcher. "We asked the administration, and they said they counted these groups as part of the black population."

A study published by the American Journal of Education shows that universities are outsourcing affirmative action. The study, carried out jointly by Princeton University and the University of Pennsylvania, based its findings on data from the National Longitudinal Survey of Freshmen. It said immigrant students are often favored, because they are highly motivated and get better grades because they can afford text preparation. It also looked at a 2004 study by Nancy Foner and George M. Fredrickson who wrote, "To white observers, black immigrants seem more polite, less hostile [and] more solicitous." The study says the nation's elite colleges and bolstering their diversity quotas with black immigrants from Africa, Latin America and the Caribbean, many of whom are wealthier, better educated, and easier to get along with than their American-born counterparts.

According to the study, 13 percent of the nation's college-age black population comes from outside the country, and at the top universities, that number approaches 25 percent. But Affirmative action intended to assist "descendant of slaves" and was never meant to be an uplifting device for socially successful blacks. . . .[5]

3.6 Invasion in Iraq (2003—) and Sunnis / Shi'ites War
The war in Iraq was sold to American public with unfounded horrors of weapons of mass destruction and the Al Qaida. Not much attention, if any at all, was

given to consequences of this international invasion, especially to possible outbreak of hostilities between the major ethnic groups in Iraq—Sunnis and Shi'ites. In the article for Time magazine Bobby Ghosh (2007) is taking a look at the roots of the struggle within Islam and whether anything can be done to stop it.

The hatred is not principally about religion. They believe in the same god. They also have a great deal in common: ethnicity, language, cusine and apparel. The ways in which they differ are subtle and vary from region to region.

Sunnis and Shi'ites are fighting for a secular prize: political domination. Since the Galiph was often the political head of the Islamic empire as well as its religious leader, imperial patronage helped make Sunni Islam the dominant sect. Today about 90% of Muslims worldwide are Sunnis.

Shi'ites see themselves as the oppressed, and they see Sunnis as the oppressors. Shi'ism would always attract some of those who felt oppressed by the empire. Shi'ites soon formed the majority in the areas that would become the modern states of Iraq, Iran, Bahrain and Azerbaijan; they are significant in Saudi Arabia, Lebanon and Pakistan.

Crucially, Shi'ites outnumber Sunnis in the Middle East's major oil-producing regions—Iran, Iraq, eastern Saudi Arabia. But outside Iran, Sunnis have historically had a lock on political power, even where Shi'ites have the numerical advantage (The one place where the opposite holds true is modern Syria, which is mostly Sunni but since 1970 has been ruled by a small Shi'ite subsect known as the Alawites.)

Sunni rulers maintained their monopoly on power by excluding Shi'ites from the military and bureaucracy; they treated Shi'ites as an underclass, limited to manual labor and denied a fair share of state resources. The rulers used religious argument to justify oppression. When Saddam killed a Sunni, it was personal—because of something that person had done, but when it came to killing Shi'ites, he was indiscriminate. He didn't need a specific reason. Their being Shi'ite was enough.

During the first post-Saddam election in January 2005 Sunni parties boycotted the poll, allowing a Shi'ite coalition to sweep to power. Shi'ites are now politically dominant in Iraq, and Iran is the leading Shi'ite power. So in most Arab capitals, the sectarian war in Iraq is increasingly blamed on Iran. Iran is backing the Shi'ite militias; Arab states sponsoring the Sunnis.

"There could be no more bitter legacy of the Bush Administration's fateful decision to go to war in Iraq," concludes Bobby Ghosh.[6]

Critical Thinking Questions

For each "case study" in the Chapter:

1. Discuss the Direction of change. For example, good intentions may lead to negative consequences; or, something positive may come up as a result of negative conditions; the consequence is neither good nor bad but a modification of the previous condition, etc.

2. Discuss the Nature of consequences—unintended, unforeseen, ironic.

3. What did go "wrong" and why? Why was the outcome unforeseen/ unintended? Was it due to ignorance, error, immediate interest, basic values, intensity of the action, etc.?

4. Discuss the Nature of an action—was it unorganized or formally organized?

Notes

1. Tyler, Lyman S., *A History of Indian Policy*. (Washington, D.C. Bureau of Indian Affairs, 1973); Lacy, Michael G., "The United States and American Indians: Political Relations" (pp. 83-104 in. *American Indian Policy in the Twentieth Century* edited by Vine Deloria, Jr., University of Oklahoma Press, 1985); Deloria, Vine, Jr. 1985. "Introduction" (pp. 3-14 in *American Indian Policy in the Twentieth Century,* edited by Vine Jr. Deloria, University of Oklahoma Press, 1985); O'Brien, Sharon, "Federal Indian Policies and the International Protection of Human Rights" (pp. 35-61 in *American Indian Policy in the Twentieth Century*, edited by Vine Jr. Deloria, University of Oklahoma Press, 1985)

2. Wax, Murray L. and Robert W. Buchanan (eds.). *Solving "The Indian Problem": The White Man's Burdensome Business*, (The New York Times Co.; 1975)

3. Gates, Henry Jr. *Op-Ed Contributor; Forty Acres and a Gap in Wealth*. The New York Time, November 18, 2007. http://www.nytimes.com/2007/11/18/opinion/18gatcs.html?r=1&orcf=slogin (accessed November 20, 2007).

4. Everet, Anna. *The Civil Rights Movement and Television*. The Museum of Broadcast Communications. February 24, 2009. http://www.museum.tv/archives/etv/C/htmlC/civilrights/civilrights.htm (accessed March 10, 2009); Nelson, Jack. "The Civil Rights Movement: A Press Perspective." *Human Rights*. Fall 2001, Vol. 28, No. 4, pp. 3-6.

5. James, Susan D. 2007. *Outsourcing Affirmative Action: Colleges Look Overseas for Racial Diversity. International Black Students Seen as "Easier to Get Along With"* file://A:\affirmative.2.htm March 8, 2007 (accessed October 23, 2008).

6. Ghosh, Bobby. "Why They Hate Each Other," *Time*, Marsh 5, 2007, pp. 29-40.

Chapter 4

Schools

4.1 Opening of Higher Education to Women, USA, 19th century

One variant of the New Woman, who emerged in the latter part of the nineteenth century, was an unintended consequence of the opening of higher education to women. The early women's colleges were to help make women better wives and mothers But in the colleges women discovered both a new world apart from their patriarchic families and new possibilities for their own achievements and self-definition. New Women used their education to pursue their own careers. Some taught in the women's colleges after graduation. Some were vocal feminists who fought for women's suffrage and other women's causes. Many continued the reform work of an earlier generation of middle-class women. Some, for example, established or participated in settlement houses in urban slums. These were community centers set up for the poor, and within them the reformers sought to better understand poverty. Here reform women, along with men reformers, sought to bring education, health care, new values, and new hope to the poverty stricken. By 1910 there were more than four hundred settlement houses in the country. These reform women developed a "sisterhood" among themselves, with a strong sense of solidarity.

The settlement houses reflected the noble ideas of reformers, but they also caused unintended class tensions: some slum dwellers resented being told by middle class reformers how to live, and some reformers were paternalistic. In the end, divisions of class undermined the reform movement.[1]

4.2 Promise Scholarship

The West Virginia PROMISE Scholarship was created in 2002 to address the problem of lack of continued education in West Virginia. Because the state was lagging behind in rates of college attendance and degrees among adults, officials wanted to provide citizens of the state the opportunity to go to college for free. They also aimed to provide an incentive for staying in West Virginia to continue education and afterwards, to encourage economic growth. The scholarship, which is merit-based, is awarded to all West Virginia students who meet the academic criteria and wish to attend a public university or college in West Virginia. Recently, there has been some debate over whether or not the scholarship is actually serving its purpose efficiently.

While the intentions of the PROMISE scholarship were completely positive, encouraging studiousness, education, and the development of the state—the goals may not be fully realized yet. According to a study performed by Marshall University and PROMISE, it does not seem that the scholarship has had a significant effect on West Virginia's retention of students and job-seekers or its ability to help less-affluent young people to attend college. According to the study—a poll given to the first graduating class of PROMISE scholars—97% of these students said that they would have attended college with or without the scholarship. 71% of them said that they would have gone to college in West Virginia. While many said that the scholarship was a major factor in keeping them in the state during their education, 21% of students did not plan to stay in the state after graduation.[2]

Debate has surfaced recently over financing the education of young people who will only leave the state. It seems that the PROMISE scholarship has facilitated the migration of many West Virginian degree-holders to other parts of the country. Citing better places to live, better money, and more jobs, these students had no plans in West Virginia. 82% of them said that the scholarship had no effect on their decision of where to begin their careers.

While the scholarship succeeded in paying for the education of many, these scholars may not be those most in need of financial assistance. Only 22% of the first graduating class were first-generation college students. Also, before the inception of the scholarship, West Virginia college-going rates had already been rising for three years. While policymakers defend the scholarship, saying that the positive effects are still in the making, it is undeniable that the scholarship is paying for the education of thousands of people who will soon move out of state. Unanticipated by these policymakers, the issue is now trying to be resolved. Changes to eligibility requirements could increase its benefit for low-income students and the creation of jobs and a better infrastructure might make the state a more attractive place to stay.

Unfortunately, educated West Virginians are emigrating at a rapid rate, leaving behind the state which helped them finance their education. The unanticipated consequences of the PROMISE scholarship are certainly not severe enough to outweigh its benefits, but changes to the system may prove beneficial for the state and for many students.

4.3 The No Child Left Behind Act of 2002

The No Child Left Behind Act of 2002 was implemented due to growing concerns about the efficacy of public education in the United States. It supplements the Elementary and Secondary Education Act of 1965 and creates new requirements that must be fulfilled by public schools in the areas of test scores, teacher quality, and a number other facets of the school system. Before the act was passed, the schools with low test scores could not be held accountable for substandard performance. The gap in accomplishment between various races and classes was also a cause for concern. These shortcomings, and many others, of public precollegiate education inspired President George W. Bush and Congress to take action to better United States schools.[3]

The enactment of this law was undoubtedly an intentional measure meant to improve education in general, especially for students who have special needs of any kind. There are mixed reactions, however, to whether or not the No Child Left Behind Act has fulfilled all of its promises. It is generally agreed that the bill has brought some positive changes, but the negative results seem to outweigh the positive. According to PBS writer Kristina Nwazota, many politicians who had been in favor of the bill now have problems with some of its provisions. Some complaints are that the act is significantly under funded and that the requirements are too difficult for many schools to meet. Another claim is that the law puts special education students at a disadvantage, rather than giving them the advantages that were intended.

In an Indiana University news release, the author cites a recent study by the Center for Evaluation and Education Policy and the Indiana Institute on Disability and Community that was the product of evaluation of a variety of national statistics as well as a survey of Indiana school administrators. This report suggests that instead of helping special education students, the bill actually presses schools to exclude these students from regular classrooms because they make it even more difficult to meet the bill's requirements. The study also shows that there is a possibility that this contributes to the rate of special education students that drop out before graduation. Because the law measures the achievements of all students according to the same guidelines, special education students are often blamed for the school failing to meet standards.[4]

4.4 Centennial "Celebration" of the System of Tracking

In the seminal article, Coleman (1968) traces the five-stage evolution of the concept of equality of educational opportunity, where the third stage is "differential curriculum." Schools may provide a differential (diverse) curriculum (college, general, vocational) which, in theory at least, allowed students, regardless of their background, to "choose" which curriculum best suited their occupational goals and interests. The comprehensive high school offered advanced academic courses, along with those in vocational and business instruction, and remedial courses in basic skills.[5]

This process was brought about largely in the early decades of the twentieth century because of increased immigrant population in the schools, economic and technological transformations, and new laws restricting child labor. In practice, of course, this is not the way it worked, for a student's home background obviously entered, then and now, into the placement (not choice) of the curriculum. Behind the policy was the assumption that all students would not benefit equally from a common education; that for many students, a classic college oriented education might be a deterrent to occupational success, especially if there was little likelihood that these students could or would attend college (ibid). Although this was an attempt to establish a greater extent of equality of educational opportunity, it led quickly to the institutionalization of "tracking" in the comprehensive high school, and soon became an expectation in elementary school as well.

Retrospectively, in view of the steady decline in student academic performance, the persistent wide gap between the educational outcomes of various subgroups in the society, and the reform efforts of the past two decades, this particular evolution of the concept may have been ill-advised (Cornelius 2004). Very little concern was expressed as to how the factors of race, gender, and social class might affect the concept of equality of educational opportunity. Looking back at almost 100 years of the practice of "tracking" the predominant consensus among scholars is that it confirmed and maintained class inequality.

Critical Thinking Questions

For each "case study" in the Chapter:

1. Discuss the Direction of change. For example, good intentions may lead to negative consequences; or, something positive may come up as a result of negative conditions; the consequence is neither good nor bad but a modification of the previous condition, etc.

2. Discuss the Nature of consequences—unintended, unforeseen, ironic.

3. What did go "wrong" and why? Why was the outcome unforeseen/ unintended? Was it due to ignorance, error, immediate interest, basic values, intensity of the action, etc.?

4. Discuss the Nature of an action—was it unorganized or formally organized?

Notes

1. Discussed in McKee, Nancy P. and Linda Stone. *Gender and Culture in America.* 3rd edition. (Cornwall-on-Hudson, NY: Sloan Publishing; 2007); Rothman, Shiela M. *Woman's Proper Place: A History of Changing Ideas and Practices, 1870 to the Present* (New York: Basic Books, 1978).

2. See also Ryan, Beth G. "Living up to the PROMISE?" *The State Journal,* January 11, 2007 [West Virginia]

3. "In Depth Coverage: No Child Left Behind." PBS, The Online News Hour, August 2005. http://www.pbs.org/newshour/indepth_coverage/education/no_child/before.html (accessed January 20, 2008).

4. *Report: No Child Left Behind is Out of Step With Special Education.* News Release, Indiana University, November 15, 2006, http://newsinfo.iu.edu/new/page/print/4379.html (accessed January 29, 2008).

5. Coleman, James S. 1968. "The Concept of Equality of Educational Opportunity," *Harvard Educational Review* 38, pp. 17-22; 1968; Cornelius, Riordan. *Equality and Achievement,* 2nd edition (Upper Saddle River, NJ, Pearson, 2004).

Chapter 5

Health Care and Delivery

5.1 The Americans with Disabilities Act of 1990

Responding to decades of discrimination and wrongful termination of disabled laborers in the United States, the Americans with Disabilities Act (ADA) was enacted in 1990. The act was meant to increase employment opportunities for the disabled and provide them with reasonable accommodations in the workplace. The purpose of the ADA, equal opportunity, has not been reached. In fact, latent consequences of the ADA have led to the employment of fewer disabled Americans.

For a variety of reasons, the ADA inhibits the growth of the disabled workforce. All of these reasons center around the idea that the ADA makes hiring individuals with disabilities less attractive to employers. To provide accommodations required by the ADA, an employer must spend money. Looming fears of lawsuits and the costs that they create are also deterrents. America's perceptions of the disabled are somewhat detrimental to their advancement as well due to media portrayals of drug abusers and the mentally ill—who actually account for 6.7% of disabled Americans protected by the ADA. Already at a disadvantage when searching for employment, the ADA gives employers one more reason to fear hiring disabled individuals.

Disabled Americans tend to occupy low-paying positions, if they work at all. They are also generally less educated than the general populace and are seen as less able, even when it comes to simple tasks. Employment decisions are made with productivity in mind. If an employer believes that an applicant is less able because they are disabled—a form of discrimination—than they will be reluctant to hire them. If they also believe that through hiring them they will incur a number of additional costs, monetary or not, a disabled person has almost no chance of being hired.

Among reasonable accommodations that are required to be provided by an employer are special tools or aid, supplemental training, changing of physical work environment, creation of new jobs, and adjusted scheduling. Accommodations tend to be more expensive for mentally disabled employees as opposed to those who are physically disabled. According to the ADA, all accommodations must be made unless the employer employs 15 people or less or the changes require "undue hardship" to the employer. While evidence shows that the monetary expenditures for these accommodations are relatively low, it does not take other corporate expenses into consideration.

Costs of legal action in cases of alleged ADA violations also can be higher than an employer is willing to incur. Even if a case is won, legal fees must be paid to fight the accusations. During 1998, 108,939 cases were put before the EEOC regarding ADA violations. Most of these cases involved termination and lack of accommodation. With all the costs (perceived and realistic) incurred by employers who hire disabled individuals, the number of people with disabilities being hired is decreasing at a significant rate. For instance, before the enactment of the ADA, 59.8% of American disabled men were employed. After the ADA, this number dropped to 48.9%. The number of employed men without disabilities dropped also, but at less than 1/3 the rate of disabled men. Empirical evidence from the Survey of Income and Program

Participation shows a direct correlation between the ADA and lower rates of employment for disabled individuals.

While the intent of the ADA was to encourage the hiring and fair treatment of people with disabilities, the opposite has been achieved. The act has created a fear amongst employers of all the possible costs of hiring and/or firing a disabled worker. Threats of litigation and requirements for a accommodation are deterring factors for employers, where originally they were envisioned as efficient forms of regulation for discrimination against the disabled. The ADA is an undeniable example of a human action stemming from basic moral and ethical logic that has been rendered virtually useless in its purpose, through its demonization amidst the corporate quest for profits.[1]

5.2 Deinstitutionalization

America has a long history of struggling with how to properly care for the severely mentally ill (SMI). Legislation began in the 1800's following Dorothea Dix's investigation of conditions for the mentally ill at the East Cambridge Jail and have continued through the 1990's. Countless efforts have been made to integrate the mentally ill into society through a process known as deinstitutionalization. In order to lower numbers of institutional patients, laws were created to release them into society and provide for outpatient treatment. Because institutional conditions have historically been cruel and often counterproductive, the efforts of lawmakers were a noble attempt at helping the mentally ill develop. Unfortunately, trends are showing that negative unanticipated consequences are outweighing any positive effects of these laws.

According the Michael Accordino article for the *Journal of Rehabilitation*, two very dominant negative consequences of deinstitutionalization are criminalization and incarceration of the SMI.[2] Because many SMI are leaving inpatient facilities with no enforced requirements for future treatment, patients often experience difficulty reintegrating into society. Because of commonly held beliefs that mentally ill individuals are always violent, dangerous, and something to be feared, another obstacle hinders their adjustment. Public hostility accompanied by lack of treatment can lead to violent or criminal outbursts and behavior patterns.

American correctional facilities are now noticing higher numbers of incarcerated SMI and longer detainment for mentally ill offenders, even for minor offenses. Some researchers say that the incarceration is being used as a quick fix for the problem of finding a place for the mentally ill. The concept of "out of sight, out of mind" allows many to justify the incarceration of the SMI as a way to keep them off the streets, or out of trouble. Imprisonment, however, is not always an effective way to correct a deviant behavior.

Recidivism has been shown to be more prevalent in mentally ill offenders. Once a sentence is completed, without the benefit of psychiatric treatment, a mentally disabled individual is bound to experience the same problems once they are released that brought them there in the first place. Other counterproductive experiences such as abuse and torment by employees and other inmates would only make it more difficult for these prisoners to return to society reformed. According to USN, "more than twice as many people with mental illness live in prisons as in state mental hospitals." The article also states that stricter punishments are often given to SMI inmates, whereas they are otherwise commonly neglected.[3]

The criminalization, incarceration, and neglect of severely mentally ill Americans are all negative unanticipated consequences of deinstitutionalization. Deinstitutionalization began as an effort to create a more positive, integrated environment for the mentally ill, but has instead had a direct impact on their high incarceration rates and continued difficulties adapting to life in society. The consequences of this process are generally thought to be completely unanticipated by those who initiated it. In the minds of those policy makers, an urgent problem needed to be solved; prompt action was necessary. They were motivated by what Merton refers to as *the factor of basic values*, by which their desire for humane treatment of mentally ill hospital patients commanded that they react to a pressing issue. A lack of planning and consideration, however, led to a situation in which virtually no intended goals were met and many unfavorable, previously unrecognized results were found.

5.3 De-industrialization and Obesity

When General Motors (GM) had closed the U.S. plants and opened new facilities in other countries where "cheap labor" exists, the immediate consequences included: displaced people from their jobs; unemployment; poverty; crime; mental health problems; the need for geographic relocation; abandoned communities; etc. Take, as an example, our home town—Huntington, West Virginia. Nearly 90,000 people lived in the city in 1950 but by 2009 the city's population has dropped to 49 thousands. From one of the major industrial cities in the beginning of Mid West it made transition to a service economy.

Probably Roger Smith, the Chair of GM, could not foresee (and did not bother to) at least one more consequence—obesity. Nearly half the adults in Huntington's five-county metropolitan area are obese—an astounding percentage, far bigger than the national average in a country with a well-known weight problem. No other metro area comes close to Huntington's adult obesity rate, according to the report by the U.S. Centers for Disease Control and Prevention, based on data from 2006.

For decades, Huntington thrived with the coal mines to its south, as barges, trucks and trains loaded with the black fuel continually chugged into and past the city. There were plenty of manufacturing jobs in the chemical industry and in glassworks, steel and locomotive parts. Obesity was not a worry then. Workplace injuries were. But as the coal industry modernized and the economy changed, manufacturing jobs left.

Culture and history are at least part of the problem, health official say.

The traditional diet was heavy with fried foods, salt, gravy, sauces, and fattier meats dense with calories burnt of through manual labor. Currently, many workers lack health insurance, and corporate wellness programs—common at large national companies—are rare.

With the poverty rate at 19 percent in 2008, much higher than the national average, many people think of healthy eating as luxuries. Fast food has become a staple, with many residents convinced they can't afford to buy healthier foods, said Keri Kennedy, manager of the state health department's Office of Healthy Lifestyles. Lack of exercise is another concern. Cultural attitude never included exercise for health.[4]

Critical Thinking Questions

For each "case study" in the Chapter:

1. Discuss the Direction of change. For example, good intentions may lead to negative consequences; or, something positive may come up as a result of negative conditions; the consequence is neither good nor bad but a modification of the previous condition, etc.

2. Discuss the Nature of consequences—unintended, unforeseen, ironic.

3. What did go "wrong" and why? Why was the outcome unforeseen/ unintended? Was it due to ignorance, error, immediate interest, basic values, intensity of the action, etc.?

4. Discuss the Nature of an action—was it unorganized or formally organized?

Notes

1. DeLeire, Thomas, "The Unintended Consequences of the Americans with Disabilities Act." Regulation 23.1, 1999; Perry, Greg, *Disabling America: The Unintended Consequences of the Government's Protection of the Handicapped* (Nelson Current, 2004).

2. Accordino, Michael P. "Deinstitutionalization of Persons with Severe Mental Illness: Context and Consequences." *Journal of Rehabilitation*, April-June, 2001.

3. Berman, Jackie, "Un-Natural Consequences." *Legal Issues in Disability* The University of Massachusetts Medical School Sep. 2000. http://www.mnipnet.org/ddlead.nsf/d0124d90f77b83c9852569a7005c7c68/d5112ad51d72b81f852569dd006de7a0!Open Document (accessed February 15, 2008); Schwartz, Emma. "A Court of Compassion." *U.S. News & World Report* 18 Feb. 2008: 39-40.

4. The story is partially based on "W. Virginia town shrugs at poorest health ranking," November 16, 2008. http://www.foxnews.com/story/0,2933,452945,00.html (accessed March 19, 2010)

Chapter 6

Government:

6.1 Welfare Reforms of the 90s
The American Welfare System began in the 1960's when the society experienced an enormous increase in financial aid from the government. According to James William Coleman and Harold R. Kerbo, "from the month of December in 1960 to the month of February in 1969 the number of AFDC (Aid to Families with Dependent Children) increased by 107 percent." Also, during the 1960's, President Lyndon B. Johnson launched a program known as the War on Poverty. More government aided programs appeared in America such as Job Corps and Head Start. Moving on through history, Welfare worked quietly in the background, making slow but steady progress, until the 1080's.

> Between 1981 and 1985 federal welfare spending dropped by 19 percent; about 400,000 families were cut from AFDC rolls with another 300,000 receiving lower benefits, food stamp rolls were reduced by about 1 million people, and 3 million children were cut from school lunch programs (ibid., p 205)

However, it would be unfair to say that the United States government quickly and abruptly ended welfare programs to many needy citizens. During the 1980s and 1990s, criticism of public welfare escalated dramatically. Some states began to experiment with programs that required welfare recipients to find work within a specified period of time, after which welfare benefits would cease.

The 1996 reform was meant to create "self-sufficiency" among welfare recipients by sending them into the workforce so that they could support themselves and would no longer have to rely on government assistance. The intent of welfare reform was initially harmless, encouraging recipients to take the steps towards independence. Unfortunately, welfare reform carried many negative unanticipated consequences with it and has still yet to reach its stated goal, at least on any wide scale. Although the welfare rolls are down, more and more American citizens are struggling to get by. Not only are they not self-sufficient; they now have no one to help them make a comfortable place for themselves in society.

The idea of self-sufficiency has been criticized for being unclear and broad. While it is generally assumed to mean that a person no longer relies on government assistance, it is not easily defined and, therefore, difficult to gauge. There are no clear terms under which to evaluate the success of welfare reform in creating self-sufficiency, therefore its effect on poverty is the only way to see its effects. Welfare reform, although well-received at first, has become an important issue in American politics and particularly in areas where poverty is prevalent (such as Appalachia). Many believe that reforms have not done their jobs, and in fact worsened the plight of impoverished Americans.

According to Sharon Hays, "A nation's laws reflect a nation's values." If this is true, according to Hays, welfare reform leaves many recipients (especially single mothers) in a position where they are unable to embody these values--the values of work and family, particularly. Welfare reform laws forced single mothers into low-paying jobs where hours are often long and children must be left in the care of others. The jobs that these women are able to attain often do not meet even minimum requirements to provide for a family, yet they are no longer able to depend on government financial assistance. Time limits are placed on their benefits and once the time is up, they are unable to receive benefits ever again. Because they are forced to find work as quickly as possible, women often take difficult jobs at minimum wages, which is particularly beneficial to employers. These employers, then, are able to exploit employees because they know that they have to sustain employment. Low wages paid to these workers also make it harder for non-welfare-to-work applicants to obtain jobs. These are just a few of the many negative unanticipated consequences of welfare reform.

Prior to the reforms of 1996, Americans generally felt as if their tax dollars were being spent on lazy welfare recipients who did not want to work. In order to quell these complaints and assist welfare recipients in becoming self-sufficient, the government agreed that a massive reorganization was necessary. This reorganization, ridden with red tape and paperwork, has caused more harm than good. The population of American working poor is growing. Without the necessary foresight, the federal government turned thousands of recipients loose, deciding that welfare should be an aid in transitional periods, not a law of life. Perhaps unanticipated by policymakers are the other factors that are necessary for individuals to succeed.

While welfare checks were not large enough to account for all expenses for most recipients, many of them had other forms of income such as friends and family or paid work. Even those with jobs, they are unable to support themselves on their income alone. For these people who once were able to rely on federal aid, the transition into "self-sufficiency" is not an easy one. It is undeniably not immediate with the acquisition of a job, and more often than not that job will never provide enough for a family. Other provisions are necessary for individuals to reach the point of independence such as social networking, soundness of neighborhoods and surroundings, logical advice, mental health, and a governmental system that works in their favor. A certain quality of life is necessary for an individual to succeed. Unfortunately, most areas inhabited by those under the poverty line are not conducive to development and progress.

A structural functionalism, according to Hawkins, is necessary for the success of the individual. A supportive and developing community with plenty of jobs and resources is essential. Temporary assistance for a few members of society does not create a positive effect unless the society is thriving and supportive as a whole. By neglecting the larger picture of welfare problems, policymakers made hasty decisions that have led to increased problems of poverty in the United States. Careful analysis of what would happen once recipients were cut off was not employed. The sense of urgency about the situation led to broad, sweeping changes that have indisputably caused much larger problems.

While the stated intent of welfare reform was to create self-sufficiency among the poor, it has not had significant success. If the true goal was to reduce the number of individuals receiving welfare benefits, however, it succeeded. What is more important than the success of government policy, though, is its direct effect on American citizens. The poor are getting poorer. Single mothers have difficulty balancing work and family, sometimes causing one of the two to fall behind. Without proper training and education, many are working minimum wage jobs. Structural shortcomings negatively affect them as well. With no guidance, less privileged schools, and growing crime rates; it is difficult to imagine how the children will rise above their current situations. More and more roadblocks refuse access to self-sufficiency, and poverty is growing. These unanticipated consequences of welfare reform that have devastated so many may have been easily avoided if policymakers would have explored the possible consequences of these reforms before they went into place.[1]

6.2 West Virginia and the New Deal

The Great Depression (1929-1940) took its toll on the entire United States, but according to Brad McElhinny (1999) of the Charleston Daily Mail, West Virginia was one of the hardest hit states in the nation.[2] According to him, the Depression had lasting effects on the state that continued long after the rest of the country was recovering. This is due, in part, to the lack of foresight by policymakers when enacting the New Deal programs that are touted as some of the most important legislation of the past century.

The country was in crisis and something needed to be done. Out of this urgent necessity came a series of programs referred to as the New Deal, designed to pull the country out of economic turmoil. While the programs accomplished many of their widely varying goals and helped many people, they surely did not solve the problem for West Virginians. West Virginia was different, and still is. The state is widely known to be "owned" by coal. The coal industry in West

Virginia is powerful and accounts for a huge portion of its revenue. Also important to West Virginians at the time was farming, particularly subsistence faring. Coal mining and farming were two of the industries that suffered the most from the Great Depression.

During the Great Depression, West Virginia elected two different governors (Governor Herman Guy Kump and Homer Adams Holt) who were reluctant to adopt New Deal policies. It is debatable of why the governors failed to match funds provided by the federal government for various projects. According to McElhinny, as fiscal conservatives, they did not want to accept debt from the national government. According to Delegate (WV) John Doyle (2009, personal communication), they turned down some federal funds because West Virginia was so poor it couldn't afford the federal matching money for all that it was allotted. Regardless, the state of West Virginia failed to take advantage of all the opportunities offered by New Deal programs. As a result, the infrastructure of West Virginia suffered. Schools and roads worsened substantially. This began a cycle of neglect that deeply hurt West Virginia economically. By neglecting the state's infrastructure, it made it an unattractive place for companies to build factories, essentially removing it from the market for employment opportunities. The state was suffering badly due to decisions made by the governors, and it would soon get worse with the enactment of the National Industrial Recovery Act.

The National Industrial Recovery Act was intended to aid the country's failing economy, but because of specific conditions in West Virginia it carried negative latent consequences. The act suspended antitrust regulation for businesses that were trying to support positive and ethical work environments. If a company set a minimum wage, maximum hours, and allowed collective bargaining; it was temporarily exempt from these laws. However well-meaning the Act was, it created major problems that lasted decades. A mass mobilization of the United Mine Workers took place and wages were raised. Seemingly positive consequences, however, were negative. Because West Virginia workers were being paid more, even fewer factories located to West Virginia. The longer the companies already there paid these wages, the more they resented it

Dependency on government assistance by both citizens and communities is a serious long-term consequence. West Virginia is still in economic despair and relies more and more on outside help. Citizens of the state are impoverished above national levels and welfare is no longer supporting them as much as it once did. While the New Deal programs did a number of positive things for the country and the state, the way it was handled in WV resulted in a serious dependency and long-term problems that are still affecting the state today.

6.3 China's One Child Policy (1979—) on Imbalance of Genders

The family planning strategies of China have been in the news for decades, since the implementation of the one child policy by Deng Xiaoping in 1979.

Originally, the policy was intended to be a temporary solution to the problem of overpopulation. China announced in 2007 that it would continue this course of action through 2010 and indefinitely). Aside from the moral concerns raised by outsiders, which have gone virtually unanswered by Chinese officials, the one child policy has created other negative ramifications.

Families who have more than one child are forced to pay a fee to the government. This fee was too much for poor families to afford but well within the reach of the more affluent Chinese until January 2007, when China announced that it would lower the fines imposed on the poor. Although the step shows an interest in the needs of Chinese citizens, public outcry continues over the fines and many are calling for a different form of punishment. Prior to this legislation, wealthy Chinese families were easily able to "buy" more than one child so that they could bypass the law. The ability of the rich to buy more children is a consequence stemming from a combination of ignorance and basic values. The ability of some to corrupt the system with money most likely was not anticipated due to a focus on a specific topic of importance—controlling the population by punishing offenders with a fine.

Although China relaxed the one-child-policy laws to a degree, its problematic family planning strategy continues to come under fire for other reasons. A major problem facing China now is an unintended consequence directly correlated to the one-child-policy as well as the traditional Chinese disparagement of women. Male babies between birth and the age of four are now outnumbering women in China at a rate of 114 to 100, as opposed to the natural rate of 105 to 100. Because women are commonly valued less than men in Chinese culture, many families find ways to ensure that their one child is a boy. In rural areas, where the imbalance is even more severe, many families feel the need to have male children so that they will have assistance in old age. Sex-specific abortion has significantly lowered the number of female births and some families resort to abandonment, neglect, or even infanticide. China's government predicts that by 2020, men will outnumber women by 30 million and the number continues to grow. This unintended consequence results from a nationwide value of males over females, therefore making it cyclical with the continuation of the one-child-policy.

Apart from the obvious negative impact of such a large gender difference are some other unforeseen consequences. The Chinese report states that the eventual imbalance of genders is a "serious hidden danger which may lead to social disorder." This refers to a fear, backed up by multiple studies, that male overpopulation will lead to higher crime rates—particularly higher rates of crimes against women such as kidnapping them to sell in the sex trade or as brides. These unintended consequences could certainly create a serious problem in China which could not have possibly been anticipated in 1979.

Despite the evidence of future negative consequences, and ones that are already taking place, China stands firm in its policy of family planning. Although the government acknowledges the problem, no tangible steps have been taken to resolve the issues caused by the one-child-policy, which remains intact. In defense of the Chinese argument, the one-child-policy has been completely effective in its original purpose. The law has been responsible for preventing over 400 million births in the last 30 years. An important factor in the discussion, however, is whether or not the success in decreasing population outweighs the failures and negative ramifications of its unintended consequences.[3]

6.4 Zimbabwe Land Redistribution of 1990s and 2000

In 1990, a wide-scale redistribution of land took place in Zimbabwe. This action is part of a serious of land disputes plaguing the country since it was freed from Great Britain's control. When Zimbabwe gained its independence in 1965, the white minority forced the black majority off fertile farmland onto land unsuitable for agriculture. In 1980 the Lancaster House Agreement informed the white farmers that in ten years, the land would be seized and redistributed by the government, providing compensation for lost land. This compensation was heavily reliant on grants from foreign nations such as Great Britain. Despite these actions, most fertile property still was in the hands of whites and affluent blacks (HCRR 2002).

Nations that contributed to Zimbabwe's land redistribution efforts began to disagree with the way that it was proceeding. In 1998, they met to urge Zimbabwe to adopt more ethical and visible redistribution processes. This only caused tension and saw no results. In 2000 President Robert Mugabe of Zimbabwe implemented the *fast-tracts* model of redistribution, which would aim to benefit 160,000 non-landowners and give commercial farms to 51,000 blacks. The process had no judicial oversight and has been criticized as inefficient. It was ruled unconstitutional in 2000, but later returned with minor policy changes (HCRR 2002).

As of 2002, white farmers still controlled the most valuable lands in Zimbabwe. Mugabe blamed Great Britain because the land disputes began during colonial rule, but Great Britain which has appropriated millions for Zimbabwe's land reform said that the land was in the wrong hands. According to BBC News, a large part of the seized land has been given to government officials and supporters. Economic problems, drought, and questionable governmental actions have brought Zimbabwe to a vulnerable point. Adding to these problems, agricultural inefficiency is threatening Zimbabwe's economy and population (BBC 2002).

Newly settles farmers are not producing at sufficient levels, according to Zimbabwe's government. The serious issues that the country now faces are a latent consequence of the *fast-tracts* redistribution of 2000, which unintentionally left Zimbabwe's farming industry in a state of confusion and disrepair. According to the IRIN, a 2007 land audit indicated that farmlands were not being used properly. Many farms are unutilized and vacant because the people that they were awarded to had not been able to claim them yet. Many farmers also have not been able to produce enough to sustain operations due to lack of fuel and supplies—a result of Zimbabwe's terrible economic plight. According to economic analyst John Robertson, those with successful farms either inherited a solid, functional farm or are government beneficiaries (IRIN 2008).

One reason Robertson believes the farms are failing is the latent motivation behind land redistribution—political gain for Mugabe. Robertson also points to irresponsible distribution without assurance of funding, guidance, or training. This lack of forethought classifies the result as an *unanticipated* consequence. The result is that new farmers, who were unprepared to take over the land, are being punished for the government's failure to analyze the circumstances of their actions beyond creating political support (IRIN 2008).

Now, these farmers are outraged. After facing droughts, financial problems, lack of experience, and frequent heavy rain seasons, they do not feel responsible for farm failures. They also point to favors given to political supporters and veterans (IRIN 2008). Veterans, however, are irate too. They vow to fight the repossession of the land that they fought for. Veteran leader Joseph Chinotimba suggests that the government take time to train farmers to be productive (talkzimbabwe.com 2008).

Whereas Mugabe may have achieved political popularity initially through the land redistribution, unforeseen consequences have arisen. Not only are these consequences negative; they are threatening the well-being of the nation. The action failed to put farmland in the hands of many people, instead giving it to political officials. Those who did receive farmland were not prepared to use it. Economic and weather-related turmoil had intensified the effects. Now, Zimbabwe is once again divided and disadvantaged, resulting from a complete lack of planning and analysis of circumstances.[4]

6.5 Changes in the Teachers Retirement Systems (TRS) since 1991 (West Virginia)[5]

In 1991, the state legislature, concerned about the growing unfunded liability in the Teachers Retirement System (TRS), created a new retirement fund for all public school teachers hired after that year. It was to be a "defined contribution" plan, as opposed to the "defined benefit" plan under the "old" fund. Teachers hired before the creation of the "new" fund had the option of joining it, or staying in the "old" one.

Many states were doing the same thing in the 1990s. The idea of "defined contribution" had become popular in the private sector, and was considered a more financially sound way of managing a retirement fund. TDC is a 401(k)-style plan. Under the "new" plan, teachers would invest their own money, rather than have the state invest it for them. They were given a choice among financial agents. Unfortunately, the choice of financial agents was to be determined by the type of investments desired by the individual contributor. If you wanted to invest in bonds, you went to one agent. Stocks? A second agent. A third agent was to invest your money in anything else.

The agent chosen to manage bonds was apparently a sweeter talker than the others. Almost all the investments were in bonds. Bonds are a surer investment than any other, but bring the smallest return. Most financial advisors tell their clients to "play the field" (balance their portfolio by investing in all types of instruments). By 2005 the legislature realized it made a mistake by not having all the financial agents permitted to invest "across the board."

Most teachers in the "new" plan now have retirement savings nowhere near the size of those in the "old" (defined benefit) plan. The state closed the program to new hires in 2005 amid complaints of insufficient returns. A number of enrollees allege they lack the funds in their accounts to retire; the average account contained under $34,000 last year.

Because the state was at least part of the reason for this deficiency, many legislators (John Doyle included) believe the state has a responsibility to subsidize, to some degree, the members of the "new" plan. This debate has occupied center stage the entire legislative session of 2008. The governor, the House of Delegates and the Senate has each come up with a plan. The three plans are very different from each other, both quantitatively and qualitatively. On Sunday, March 16, 2008 both houses passed the bill—HB4623 (Retirement contributions)—giving teachers in the "new" system the option of moving into the 'old" one. However, the conditions the legislature placed on the people who would be moving are somewhat difficult.

The bill would allow voluntary transfers into the Teachers Retirement System by TDC enrollees if at least 65 percent move; with about 19,000 TDC members, at least 12,300 would have to transfer. But as those enrollees have been paying less of their salaries than what this other program requires, they would face differing payments to receive its full benefits. If between 65 percent and 75 percent transfer, these payments would range between $1,000 and $40,500. If more than 75 percent move, they would face payments of between $900 and $11,843.

The latter payments are calculated from 1.5 percent of salary, plus interest. It also relies on $24.5 million in state funds to cover the cost of providing the benefits, which are based on years of service and final salary.

According to Delegate John Doyle, "it's up in the air whether what we did in the just completed session will solve the problem."

6.6 Annexation of Unincorporated Areas (West Virginia)[6]

Annexation of unincorporated areas by municipalities has always been a hot topic in West Virginia. The pickle in which we find ourselves is a classis example of the "law of unintended consequences."

For many years, it was extremely difficult for cities in West Virginia to annex unincorporated areas. The West Virginia County Commissioners' Association liked that situation, and the West Virginia Municipal League, of course, hated it. The Municipal League kept trying to get the legislature to make annexation easier, and the Commissioners' Association always dug in its heels.

No change was made to annexation laws until the County Commissioners discovered what they thought was a flaw: towns were using the "minor boundary adjustment" to annex areas that were clearly more than "minor." Generally, there are three ways to annex: first, the "election" method calls for a referendum in both the annexing municipality and the folks the area to be annexed; second, the "petition" method calls a petition signed by a majority of the folks in the area to be annexed and a vote of the governing body of the annexing city; third, the "minor boundary adjustment" is essentially the use of the petition method when there is only one piece of property to be annexed.

Up until a half dozen years ago, both the election and petition methods could only be used to annex areas that met a very strict "density" requirement. It was so strict that if, say, Fairmont and Old Prospect streets (bordering Shepherdstown on the south) wanted to be annexed, they would have been forbidden by law from having that happen.

But, when a few towns began using the minor boundary adjustment to take in large pieces of open land, the County Commissioners' Association took note. It seems that county commissions had no control over that action.

So, the County Commissioners' Association agreed with the Municipal League on a compromise: the county commission of each county would have veto power over annexation by minor boundary adjustment, and the "density" requirement would be removed from the other two methods. The legislature passed this compromise into law.

This leads us to the first round of unanticipated consequences. In short order, the County Commissioners realized they had been snookered. They had not anticipated that the "petition" method would be used to take in large individually or family owned parcels of land. This method essentially replaced the minor boundary adjustment as the method towns used to expand their territory.

What has made the situation unbearable is the habit of a few municipalities to use the "petition" method to annex large parcels of land that are not really "contiguous." State law requires that any annexation be contiguous, but it doesn't define the term very clearly. The cities like Ranson annex state roads that lead to a property as part of the annexation of that property. This is called "pipe stem" or "shoestring" annexation. This type of annexation, which according to Delegate John Doyle, should be stopped, leads us to the second round of unanticipated: it enables a town to get more real estate property taxes initially, without having to provide much in the way or services. However, in the long run, it is going to cost the citizens of the original part of the municipality more, because the service that will have to be provided to the annexed area (once it is developed) will be quite costly. Why? City employees (police, firefighters and other kinds of municipal servants) will have to travel some distance over land that is essentially not in the town to provide the services.

6.7 Congressional and State Legislative Redistricting (West Virginia)[7]

Congressional and state legislative redistricting must be done every ten years to conform to the most recent population figures in the decennial census.

Some may suggest that packing greater percentages of minority population into certain district increases the chance of electing minorities to congress and state legislatures. However, that means there will be fewer districts with significant minority populations. So, the representatives of those other districts will have less incentive to listen to the policy concerns of minorities. Thus, more minority representative means less representation of minority interests.

If a given minority has most of its people put into districts where they form a majority, it will have the greatest possible percentage of its members elected to office. However, if that same minority saw its people spread among twice as many districts, it will have fewer of its members elected to office, but will have significant influence over the behavior of a greater number of elected representative. This is because the representative of any legislative district pays very serious attention to the desires of any group forming a significant portion of his/her district, even if that group is less than a majority of the district.

Critical Thinking Questions

For each "case study" in the Chapter:

1. Discuss the Direction of change. For example, good intentions may lead to negative consequences; or, something positive may come up as a result of negative conditions; the consequence is neither good nor bad but a modification of the previous condition, etc.

2. Discuss the Nature of consequences—unintended, unforeseen, ironic.

3. What did go "wrong" and why? Why was the outcome unforeseen/ unintended? Was it due to ignorance, error, immediate interest, basic values, intensity of the action, etc.?

4. Discuss the Nature of an action—was it unorganized or formally organized?

Notes

1. See Coleman, James W. and Harold R. Kerbo, *Social Problems* 9th ed. (Upper Saddle River, NJ: Pearson Education; 2006); Hawkins, Robert L. "From Self-Sufficiency to Personal and Family Sustainability: A New Paradigm for Social Policy." *Journal of Sociology and Social Welfare* (2005). http://findarticles.com/p/articles/mi_m0CYZ/is_4_32/ai_n1641862 (accessed March 1, 2008); Hays, Sharon, *Flat Broke With Children* (New York: Oxford University Press, 2004).

2. McElhenny, Brad, "The Depression Came Early and Stayed Long in Coal-Dependent W.Va." *Charleston Daily Mail* 6 Apr., 1999; Messina, Lawrence, "Legislators pass budget worth $3.9B," *The Helard-Dispatch*. March 17, 2008, 1A, 4A

3. See also Rosenberg, Matt, "China's One Child Policy: One Child Policy in China Designed to Limit Population Growth." About.com. 7 Oct. 2007. 1 Feb. 2008 http://geographyabout.com/od/populationgeography/a/onechild.hp=1 (accessed February 1, 2008); Fan, Maureen, "China May Lower Fines for Poor Who Violate One-Child-Only Policy." *Washington Post* 24 Jan. 2007; Vause, John. "China Doomed for Bachelorhood?" Sify 1 Feb. 2007_[India] . http://sify.com/news/fullstory.php?id=14379936 (accessed February 1, 2008).

4. "War Vets on Warpath With Government Over Decree on Land" TalkZimbabwe.com 15 Feb. 2008 http://www.talkzimbabwe.com/print.php?a=1629 (accessed February 15, 2008); "Who Owns the Land?" *BBC News*. 8 Aug. 2002. 11 Feb. 2008 http://news.bbc.co.uk/2/hi/africa/594522.stm (accessed February 11, 2008); "Zimbabwe Government and Farmers Locked in Land Reform Dispute." *Human and Constitutional Rights Resource*. 1 Dec. 2002 http://www.hrcr.org/hottopics/zimbabwe.html (accessed February 11, 2008): "Zimbabwe: New Land Owners Face Eviction." IRIN 11 Feb. 2008. 11 Feb. 2008 http://www.irinnews.org/Report.aspx?ReportId=76682 (accessed February 11, 2008).

5. This part is based on contribution by Delegate John Doyle (WV House of Delegates)

6. This part is based on contribution by Delegate John Doyle (WV House of Delegates)

7. This part is based on contribution by Delegate John Doyle (WV House of Delegates)

Chapter 7

Environment

Human impact on the environment is undeniable. Over the past few decades, more and more attention has been given to the human decisions and actions that are degrading our landscape every day. Policy and private actions have caused devastating affects across the world and in our atmosphere. Often, these effects are unforeseen, or at least unintended. The unintended consequences of our actions can range from very small impacts to very large ones. Unfortunately, when it comes to environmental issues, unintended consequences are rarely positive. Problems such as climate change are a result of the actions of millions of people over long periods of time. However, sometimes it is just the action of a single individual that can have stunning consequences on the environment.

7.1 Release of Domestic European Rabbits in Australia in 1859

The first domestic European rabbits were brought to Australia with the First Fleet in 1788, but the population did not begin to flourish and create unforeseen consequences until after 1859. That year, Thomas Austin released twenty four of the animals at Barwon Park in Victoria. Austin was an avid hunter who regularly devoted his weekends to rabbit hunting while he was living in Europe. To his disappointment, there were no native rabbits to be found in Australia. To solve this problem, he brought two dozen rabbits, along with a number of birds, near his home so that he could continue his beloved sport. Unfortunately, Austin had no way of predicting the devastating effect that the rabbits would soon have on Australia's landscape and economy.

According to Tim Bloomfield of the Department of Primary Industries in Victoria, some farmers were already beginning to desert their lands in 1881. Ten billion rabbits had infested Australia by 1926, and the population was continuing to grow at rapid rates. The flat areas of ground vegetation were a perfect breeding ground for the newly introduced species. Humans were directly responsible for the release of the rabbits, and furthermore they had unknowingly prepared a perfect landscape for their occupation.

Australia's ecosystem was impacted so heavily by the growing number of rabbits that more notice began to be taken to the conditions of the area's flora and fauna. Because rabbits constantly move around in search of an optimal feeding and breeding area, they are able to destroy vast areas of landscape within a short period of time. Rabbits are actually able to completely purge a pasture of all grass, providing room for weeds and other less-desirable ground-covering plants to spring up. According to Bloomfield, this incredible ability also leads to soil erosion, which—among other problems—can lead to the contamination of water sources. Aside from direct effects on Australia's terrain, rabbits also placed a previously unknown amount of stress on native wildlife.

Since the introduction of the rabbits, over one-eighth of all mammalian species in Australia became extinct. Decreased amounts of vegetation, directly caused by the rabbit infestation, led to a competition among native animals for this primary food source. Rabbits are even attributed as a large cause in the jeopardizing of the Greater Bilby and the Pig-Footed Bandicoot, two animals once common to Australia that are now threatened and nearing extinction, according to Bloomfield. Because rabbits are able to reproduce so quickly and alter the environment so much, they pose a serious threat to other species. Two rabbits can procreate resulting in 184 of the animals in a period of only eighteen months. With this competition for food and resources, as well as the alteration of their natural environment, many native Australian species have been negatively affected by the introduction of European rabbits. The rabbits have also provided overabundance of food for predators such as foxes, who have been able to thrive in numbers as a result. The increased numbers of predators is also affecting native mammals, as they are much more likely to become prey than before.

Beyond the effects on Australia's native plant and animal life, European rabbits have wreaked economic havoc on the nation. Australian wool production was devastated by the introduction of rabbits. Through the rabbits' elimination of pastures, farmers face troubling circumstances when trying to maintain lands for their sheep to graze. Although Bloomfield says that it has been difficult to record the precise effects of rabbits on wool productivity due to varying conditions. He claims, however, that "the real extent of earlier economic losses was clearly revealed by the enormous increase in wool and meat production which followed myxomatosis, successfully introduced in the early 1905s" (Bloomfield 1999). Myxomatosis is one of many methods that Australians have employed to try to rid the country of rabbit infestation. Although many techniques have been developed in an attempt to eradicate the rabbit population in Australia, nothing has been entirely successful. Because it is so difficult to exterminate rabbits at a faster rate than they can multiply, the task of completely eliminating them from the Australian ecosystem seems nearly impossible.

Rabbits were declared to be an established pest with the passage of the Catchment and Land Protection Act of 1994 and groups all over the country are fighting the infestation today. These rabbits are still a source of frustration and economic and ecological problems almost 150 years after Thomas Austin introduced them. Austin's seemingly innocent attempt to bring his favorite European pastime with him to the new colony has had resounding unintended and unforeseen consequences that have devastated Australia ever since.[1]

7.2 Fence Construction Along US—Mexican Border

While Australians have been battling the problem of rabbit overpopulation for nearly 150 years, some American have been battling to keep a few remaining jaguars in its rural southwest region in recent years. The unintended consequence of introducing rabbits into a foreign ecosystem has been detrimental to its residents. Conversely, some residents of the American Southwest fear that an unintended consequence of U.S. immigration policy could be detrimental to their environment by denying them the chance to catch a glimpse of a once-native, elusive creature that has only recently resurfaced on American soil.

The American jaguar once wandered the Southwest freely, until the twentieth century when the large cats were trapped and killed out of existence to make room for the large ranches that now dominate the landscape. In 1996, however, a mountain lion hunter named Warner Glenn made an astonishing discovery when he was out on a hunt in Arizona. What Glenn discovered, and consequently photographed, was actually a jaguar. Glenn's photographs are thought to be the first of a live jaguar in U.S. history. Shortly after Glenn's first sighting, a mountain lion tracker named Jack Childs spotted another jaguar. Child caught his finding on videotape. Since 1996, only a few male jaguars have been spotted in the United States, and according to a CNN article, they are not permanent residents of the area but visitors.[2] One way or another, the sightings have inspired environmentalists and others and have caused a significant amount of debate over the fate of the American jaguars.

Illegal immigration from Mexico to the United States is a controversial topic and has been the subject of many new laws and actions by the U.S. Department of Homeland Security in recent years. According to a Reuters article, the U.S. government plans to complete 670 miles of barriers across the border between the two countries by the end of 2008. The plan is aimed at curbing the high numbers of illegal immigrants who make their way across these high-traffic areas by foot or by vehicle each year. According to jaguar biologist Emil McCain, this will make it impossible for these few jaguars that have been sighted to survive.

The nearest population of jaguars is over one hundred miles south of the border and no females have been spotted in the U.S. "Because there are no females and no reproduction, jaguars in the United States are totally dependent on cross-border movement. . . . " he says, "The connectivity with Mexico is absolutely crucial."

Unfortunately, the United States government does not seem to be sympathetic to the situation. According to CNN, they have already set aside 30 environmental laws to build the border barriers in the first place. While the article says that Homeland Security continues to talk to residents of the area about their opinions, the project has moved ahead despite complaints and even a lawsuit filed by Kieran Suckling of the Center for Biological Diversity, which asks that the U.S. Fish and Wildlife Service initiate a program to protect the jaguars and encourage their growth. According to a memorandum signed by Director Dale Hall of the Fish and Wildlife Service, there is not a significant enough population of jaguars north of the border to warrant U.S. protection. It states that the protection efforts should be undertaken by authorities in Mexico and South America, where the number of jaguars is larger. Warner Glenn disagrees: "It would be a loss to me that maybe my granddaughter or my daughter wouldn't be able to see one like I have," he says, "It's just an animal that's a beautiful, magnificent cat and they're having a little bit of trouble surviving. But they're doing it, and I would have to see us do anything that would cause the survival of that cat to go backwards."

According to an article from the New York Times, other nomadic species will also be negatively affected by the extension of the border fence, which continues to block off the pathways through which various species travel constantly. In spite of the work of conservationists to protect the jaguars on both sides of the border, the United States stands by its decision to abandon any efforts to preserve a sustainable environment for the jaguars. Even though the jaguars in the U.S. make up less than one percent of their population as a whole, those who oppose the continuation of the border fence see these policies as detrimental to more than just the jaguar population. Emil McCain says "The jaguar is a great emblem of wildness and an example of a healthy ecosystem . . . It really inspires people and creates a sense of wonder at the natural world. And in today's world, we really need that."[3]

7.3 Electronic Waste (E-Waste)

As technology is constantly improving at rapid speed in the developed world, this advancement is producing an unanticipated result that is quickly becoming a worldwide problem. Electronics, particularly computers, become virtually obsolete within a few years of their inception—a phenomenon known as Moore's Law. The progress of technology is making life more convenient for many Americans and encouraging research, but it is also creating an incredible amount of electronic waste. E-waste, as it is called, is becoming a serious problem in the United States and around the world.

The United States creates more e-waste than any other country in the world, much of which fills landfills across the nation. But the amount of waste is growing constantly. The EPA reported that in 2005, the United States created between 1.5 and 1.9 million tons of electronic waste. Politicians and policy-makers have started to urge for recycling legislation to control the problem. This push to reuse e-waste has caused another unanticipated consequence, however. Much of this "recycled" e-waste (around 50-80%) is being shipped East to nations such as China, India, and Ghana, where it is having dangerous effects.

Of particular concern to many is not the excess waste, but what it contains. Discarded electronics contain toxins and carcinogens such as lead and mercury that cause serious health problems. These toxins can contaminate land, water, or air. Workers in countries like Ghana are being exposed to these elements all day as they tear apart United States electronic waste to remove recyclable materials. Federal prison inmates, employed by Dell, experience the same thing in America.

China has received a particularly large amount of e-waste from the West, offering laborers there decent profits from recycling scrap metals. The sales or receipt of e-waste was banned in China in 2000, but in 2002 a scathing documentary "Exporting Harm" surfaced showing the extremely dangerous conditions in which Chinese laborers were still working. According to *National Geographic*, the film showed "entire families, from young to old—engaged in dangerous practices like burning computer wire to expose copper, melting circuit boards in pots to extract lead and other metals, or dousing the boards in powerful acid to remove gold." Chinese scientists have reported frightening information about contamination around electronic salvage areas. Everything from the soil to human blood was found to be contaminated when they studied Guiyu, the site featured in the film. After the release of the documentary, China began a much stricter enforcement of e-waste laws. According to David N. Pellow, ethnic studies professor at the University of California San Diego, however, stricter policies in some countries will not stop the e-waste problem. Pellow says, "The flow simply shifts as it takes the path of least resistance to the bottom." It will take the cooperation of all nations, including the largest exporter of e-waste, the United States, to enforce worldwide e-waste regulations.

Another unanticipated consequence of technology's advancement and the problem of e-waste may hit a little closer to home for American policymakers. "The U.S. right now is shipping large quantities of leaded materials to China, and China is the world's major manufacturing center," chemist Jeffrey Weidenhamer says. While the U.S. was trying to keep the e-waste problem out of the public eye, U.S. was contributing to the contamination of many materials that were being sent directly back to America as finished products. There seems to be a direct correlation between the contamination of China's soil, water, or air by electronic waste toxins (such as lead) and the high lead content in Chinese products which has recently been publicized.[4]

In the advancement of technology, consumers reap many benefits. Unanticipated consequences of the rapid growth of technology, however, are causing a lot of problems. In the interest of advancing science and technology, the United States has become dangerously wasteful with their electronics, causing the possible contamination of soil, water, or air and the disease or death of humans around the world and at home.

7.4 Mountaintop Removal

Degradation of the environment is both a short-term and long-term unintended consequence of many human actions. While the progress of electronic technology is indirectly poisoning land, water, air, and even human blood, new advancements in coal mining technology are directly poisoning these things as well. Mountaintop removal's unintended consequences were arguable *not* unforeseen, but continue to devastate the landscapes and citizens of the United States, particularly in the region of Appalachia.

Mountaintop removal has emerged as a lucrative and advanced form of coal mining in Appalachia over the last two decades. The process, which clears mountains of foliage and blasts off their tops piece by piece, has affected mountains throughout West Virginia, Kentucky, and Tennessee. The mining industry experienced a downturn following environmental complaints and lawsuits in the late 1990s. President Bill Clinton, calling for more oversight, began a project to trace the effects of mountaintop removal. Before the study had been completed and its results had been reported, President George W. Bush entered office in 2000 and Clinton's plans were put to a halt. Changes in mining regulation imposed by the Bush administration have encouraged industry growth while unintentionally creating numerous negative consequences. These consequences cannot be classified as unanticipated, however, due to the extensive and reliable evidence and predictions about mountaintop removal's devastating effects that are well-known to policymakers and politicians today.[5]

Before mountaintop removal, mines were able to retrieve approximately 70% of the coal in a mine, whereas the new process nets 100%. Also, while new mining jobs pay well, there are significantly less of them available. Mountaintop removal undeniably, though, brings with it very large sums of money. West Virginia is widely considered to be betrothed to and controlled by the coal industry. Campaign donations and support from industry leaders encourage West Virginia politicians as well as federal politicians to relax the standards for mining. Increasing revenue and the severity of energy concerns have only furthered the industry's goals of high profit margins, power, and political influence. Its publicized intentions of creating clean, efficient energy requiring little effort or dependence on foreign nations have perhaps also materialized. The unintended and negative consequences of mountaintop removal, however, are serious and complicate the issue of coal as an optimal energy source.

The advancement of mountaintop removal is a result of small regulation changes by the Bush administration to relax mining laws. The "fill rule" of 2002, for instance, allowed mountaintop removal sites to dump waste into streambeds by renaming the debris "fill" instead of "waste". To ensure that operations run smoothly for coal companies, lawmakers weaken definitions and verbiage to allow previously illegal mining practices. These changes seem to frame hazardous mining procedures as incidental rather than irresponsible.

Environmental concerns about mountaintop removal cannot be ignored. It has destroyed approximately 5% of West Virginia's forests and filled streambeds with dangerous chemicals and silt. According to a federal study, within ten years the affected area will be larger than the state of Rhode Island. Huge areas of wilderness have already been cleared. Over 200 animal species are being affected. Selenium, a toxin poisonous to fish, is being released into Appalachian rivers. Valley fills, miles long and hundreds of feet deep, remain filled with tons of rock and debris. Results of a 2004 poll show that a two-to-one majority of Appalachians are opposed to mountaintop removal.

While the true motives of relaxed mountaintop removal laws cannot be known for sure, the industry is surely maximizing its profits. Apparently intending to create a powerful alternative fuel source, policymakers and industry leaders are continuing towards their goal. They have made many achievements along the way. Unfortunately and unintentionally, these achievements create consequences that are devastating Appalachian land, streams, and lives.

7.5 Global Warming

Arguably the most prominent negative unintended consequence which affects the environment today is climate change, or global warming. The theory of global warming has been debated fiercely in recent years but is recognized as fact by the United States Environmental Protection Agency. According to the EPA, "greenhouse gases" released through deforestation and the burning of fossil fuels are being trapped in our atmosphere, inhibiting its ability to release heat into space. Activities of everyone's daily lives depend on the electricity and fuels which contribute to the emissions of these greenhouse gases, but recent legislation is taking action to lower emissions and protect our atmosphere. At the forefront of the fight to stop global warming is Al Gore, whose film "An Inconvenient Truth," released in 2006, attempts to open our eyes to the devastation that can be caused by global warming and what we can do to stop it. While many disagree with the political nature of Gore's arguments, his message is one of importance to the future of the planet. Climate change, itself an unintended consequence of human actions, possibly leads to other far-reaching negative consequences in the environment.

According to Science Daily, coral reefs are one part of nature that is definitely affected by global warming. A study conducted by the Institut de Recherche pour le Developpement in Paris has shown a direct correlation between rising ocean temperatures linked to global warming and the degradation of coral reefs through bleaching and eventual death. This degeneration of the reefs leaves them open to colonization by the cyanobacteria that cause ciguatera, in turn poisoning the food supply of the fish who live there and eventually the humans who eat them.

The human poisoning is a result of eating exotic fish that feed on smaller algae-eating fish in areas where toxic algae grows on these damaged reefs. According to Donald M. Anderson, director of the Coastal Ocean Institute at the Woods Hole Oceanographic Institution in Massachusetts, "worldwide, we have a much bigger problem with toxins from algae in seafood than we had 20 or 30 years ago" (Casey 2007). While Casey's article says that ciguatera poisoning is recorded as far back as Homer's "Odyssey," there is substantial evidence to cite regarding recent surges in fish poisoning and their connection to global warming and pollution.

The poisoning was primarily found in areas of the South Pacific and the Indian Ocean before, but recently is popping up in the U.S., Europe, and a larger portion of Asia. Hawaii has been affected significantly by the poisoning over the past three decades, increasing 500% since the 1970s. As the demand for exotic fish grows across the world, the incidents of ciguatera are increasing at an alarming rate.

As is evident in the case of ciguatera poisoning resulting from the degradation of the world's coral reefs, global warming affects virtually every part of our environment. Its devastating effects are causing not only the depletion of natural wonders, but also medical problems in humans associated with this depletion. According to Science Daily, on the French Polynesian island of Raivavae, the poisoning itself is not the only problem. "For these fishing communities . . . global warming could be expressed not only by a degradation of their fishing grounds but also by the emergence of cardiovascular diseases linked to too rapid a transition in diet," the article says. Because the food source that they have relied on for so long is no longer safe, they are forced to dramatically alter their eating habits. This is just one example of the damage that global warming can cause, but illustrates an important connection between our environment and our survival. Climate change is threatening this vital link.

The unintended consequences of the burning of fossil fuels and unforeseen creation of greenhouse gases that have led to global warming have already started to wreak havoc on the atmosphere and human quality of life. While many people may not feel that they are experiencing any negative effects from decades of environmental harm, they are. For some however, like the islanders of Raivavae, these effects have changed their environment significantly and without notice, disrupting their very way of life. Through effects such as the rising occurrences of ciguatera poisoning across the world, though, many are experiencing these consequences more than they may realize.

7.6 Use of Wind Turbines and Wind Energy

Concerns about global warming and its effects have created a sense of urgency in the U.S. and elsewhere to develop cleaner, more environmentally-friendly forms of energy. Processes such as mountaintop removal and the burning of fossil fuels, as well as the excessive consumption of gasoline have been harming the world we live in for a long time and the ramifications have become more severe and more apparent. To address these problems, scientists and policymakers have been working hard to develop ways to reduce the negative and unforeseen consequences of the past and present by creating new resources for energy in the future. While generally speaking the positives usually outweigh the negatives in these new advancements, they too unfortunately bring some unintended and undesirable consequences.

As the energy crisis continues to worsen in America, the nation is searching for a viable answer to the problem of obtaining clean, cost-efficient energy sources. One relatively new proposal to deal with the problem is the use of wind turbines and wind energy. Although currently wind energy only accounts for .3% of energy use in the United States, it is the fastest growing renewable energy source. Some states are imposing regulations requiring that a certain percentage of energy for operations comes from renewable energy such as wind energy and steps are even being made to create similar federal regulations. With the use of wind power, however, comes a few unanticipated consequences that are a source of concern for some environmental groups and scientists.

There are currently six wind energy plants in Appalachia and fifteen in development stages. If all plans are carried out, Appalachia will be the home to approximately 1,000 wind turbines. While many environmentalist groups tout wind energy as a fantastic substitute to the "dirty" energy of coil and oil, others see too many negative environmental consequences for wind energy to be as beneficial as hoped. Of particular concern is the fatality rate of bats and birds who frequently collide with the spinning turbines. The turbines also cause changes in the migration habits of songbirds, who migrate at night close to mountaintops, unable to see the giant turbines.

Aesthetics and tourism are also negatively affected by the large turbines, which many claim are an eyesore. While many of the direct consequences of the wind turbines have not been determined, and their use is not yet extensive across Appalachia, problems are being acknowledged by many who study the renewable energy source. Most studies on wind power have been done in the West, but the effects are definitely being seen in Appalachia. Bats, for instance, are experiencing high fatality rates and as a species are not easily able to overcome these fatalities. Most of these bats have been proven to die while the turbines are moving at slow speeds, implying that the bats are just investigating the slow-moving machines and are hit and killed. Some endangered species birds and Birds of Conservation Concern have been killed as well.

Habitats and forest environments are also damaged by the construction of these turbines and their effect on where animals are able to sustain themselves. By directing species away from the turbines, they are affecting the natural ecosystem of Appalachian forests. While all energy sources create some negative consequences, many residents of Appalachia see wind power as a serious threat.

The production of wind energy is useful and achieves its original purpose, but also brings with it a number of seemingly unavoidable environmental dangers. Proponents of wind energy claim that these negative consequences are far outweighed by those of coal, but the fact remains that this particular source of energy does not come without its own set of difficulties and debates.[7]

7.7 Introduction of Hybrid Cars and the Use of Ethanol as a Fuel

The negative consequences of wind energy are already being seen in Appalachia and the rest of the country, but are arguably less devastating to the environment than those of other sources of energy which are nonrenewable and probably have much graver effects on human lives. Still, however, policymakers and citizens cannot ignore possible or probable negative consequences when new ideas are proposed. Another example of an attempt to remedy problems of constant environmental degradation at the hands of humans, particularly in the U.S., is the use of "environmentally-friendly" vehicles in place of traditional ones, which run purely on gasoline. This is another noble effort to curb environmental harm caused by the activities of our daily lives; yet it too brings with it many unintended and possibly unforeseen consequences.

In response to concerns over air quality, the pollution created by vehicles is now the subject of great debate. Two remedies to the vehicle pollution problem have become increasingly popular among environmentally-conscious drivers: hybrid cars and the use of ethanol as a fuel. Hybrid cars combine the use of gasoline engines and batteries like those used in electric cars. While not forcing consumers to constantly recharge batteries, they seem to be a much more convenient alternative to cars that run purely on electricity. Hybrids rely on battery power for the most part. The gasoline engine comes into play when the car is coasting, allowing the battery to recharge. While the use of hybrid cars may seem to be a great way to reduce fuel emissions and keep drivers from having to make major changes in their daily routines, they do present some negative unintended consequences. The biggest concern for many critics of hybrid technology is its safety for pedestrians as well as drivers and passengers.

According to an article in the Los Angeles Times, the National Federation of the Blind has been lobbying for the enactment of laws to protect blind pedestrians from hybrids. According to the article, hybrids create very little noise, making them a definite threat to pedestrians crossing the street. This is particularly true for the blind. The article states that a study at the University of California at Riverside has shown that hybrids traveling at lower speeds must be 40%

closer to pedestrians than regular motor vehicles to create enough noise for them to be detected and avoided. According to Marc Maurer, president of the NFB, no cases have yet been reported of accidents involving pedestrians who could not hear the quiet hybrid motor. He contends, however, that the danger is imminent. Ways to increase the noise produced by hybrids are being researched to mend the problem, but the threat remains. Hybrids that are already on the roads continue to be a danger to those not able to detect them when crossing streets. Another possible problem stemming from hybrid technology creates safety concerns for drivers rather than pedestrians.

In addition to a regular gasoline engine, electrical currents are responsible for powering hybrid vehicles. These currents produce electromagnetic fields that may cause serious health problems for those exposed to them, according to an article in the New York Times. While electromagnetic fields (EMFs) are present in almost every part of our daily lives, running through common appliances and cell phones, driving for extended periods of times leaves drivers and passengers susceptible to their negative effects for much longer than they would be when using a hairdryer, for example. Batteries and power cables are frequently located in close proximity to vehicle occupants as well, causing increased risk. According to the article, long-term exposure to EMFs has been recognized as dangerous by the National Institutes of Health and the National Cancer Institute and research is being done in their link to cancer and other health risks. Still, there are no federal regulations in place to standardize a safe or acceptable level of EMF exposure. This has not kept hybrid owners from performing their own tests.

Using hand-held field-strength detection meters, some owners and potential buyers have tested hybrids and found disturbing results. According to some manufacturers and experts, however, these results are not always measured correctly or with the right tools and are often unreliable. While some manufacturers such as Honda claim that their own testing has shown no danger for occupants, no standardized method has been developed to settle the debate. According to one Staten Island woman, nonetheless, her hybrid definitely made her sick. Neysa Linzer, 58, claims that she fell asleep while driving and experienced blood pressure increases while driving the Honda Civic Hybrid that she purchased to use for her job, which required driving about 200 miles per week When she requested extra shielding to protect her from harmful EMFs, Honda refused. The company stated that their hybrids were thoroughly tested for dangerous EMFs and absolved themselves of any responsibility. While no hard evidence is available to prove the direct impact of EMFs in hybrid vehicles on their occupants, the connection is scientifically feasible. According to Lawrence Gust, an expert who specializes in EMFs and electrical sensitivity, "I get a lot of clients who ask if they should buy hybrid electric cars, and I say the jury is still out." Aside from hybrid cars, the use of alternative fuels has been proposed as an efficient way to lower greenhouse gas emissions produced by gasoline engine vehicles.

Ethanol, a renewable fuel source made from corn, has been in headlines for years as the future of America's fuel independence. It is produced domestically and is completely renewable. It also emits less pollution when used to power motor vehicles, seemingly having a greatly reduced negative impact on the environment and Earth's atmosphere. While there are numerous advantages to the use of ethanol, it unfortunately is not as harmless and efficient as it may seem. One factor that limits ethanol's benefits for the environment is the production process that creates it.

As corn grows, it absorbs carbon dioxide from the atmosphere. After it is converted into ethanol and burned, it releases this carbon dioxide back into the atmosphere in the form of harmful emissions. The farming processes used to cultivate the corn also involve the use of large farm equipment that also releases harmful emissions. Ethanol also undergoes a distilling process which relies on electricity generally produced by coal, which also has adverse effects on the atmosphere. While the use of ethanol still lowers harmful emissions by about thirteen percent, according to a study at the University of California at Berkeley, this number could be much higher. According to the study, the use of cellulosic materials like switchgrass to produce ethanol could greatly increase the benefits of ethanol as a fuel source.

The production of ethanol has also caused negative unintended consequences for people who do not even benefit from its use. Enormously increased production of corn to make ethanol has resulted in soaring food prices. According to the Christian Science Monitor, protestors stormed the streets of Mexico City in 2006 in response to soaring tortilla prices, reaching over 300% the normal rate. The public outcry forced President Felipe Calderon to cap prices of the product, an indispensable part of the Mexican diet. Rising food prices can be attributed to a number of ethanol-related factors. One fundamental problem is the immense amount of land necessary for its production, which leaves less farmland available for the cultivation of other crops. The rising cost of corn-based food for livestock has also led to a price increase of meat and dairy products. Through heavy promotion by the government and other groups, ethanol's popularity has risen to great heights. This popularity, though it may signal a small shift in gasoline consumption and environmental responsibility, cannot be categorized as completely beneficial for humanity or our surroundings.

Beyond the negative environmental effects associated with ethanol and its effect on those who do not utilize it, it also has unintended effects on the consumer. The price and availability of ethanol varies greatly from place to place. Most ethanol in the U.S. is produced in the Midwest, where prices are generally lower than those of gasoline. In other parts of the country, however, the price is often even higher than that of gasoline. Also, even if ethanol is readily available to you and cheaper than gasoline, you will be getting less power for your money. Ethanol produces less energy than gasoline and lowers fuel economy by twenty to thirty percent. Essentially, even at the best prices, ethanol may still be less attractive to the consumer than gasoline. Also, the standard gas tank is only able to use 10% ethanol without damage to seals and gaskets. Special materials are required to prevent this damage, generating extra costs for any consumer that wants to maximize their use of renewable fuel. Considering the cost-benefit ratio of ethanol for the consumer, the benefit may still prevail. Undoubtedly, the lack of availability and unforeseen costs associated with ethanol use may not give consumers the deal that they bargained for.

As the US attempts to curb its appetite for oil and reduce its impact on the environment, new technologies offer exciting opportunities for consumers to do their part. Unfortunately, with every advancement come disadvantages. Hybrid vehicles and the use of ethanol are just two recent steps in the struggle for fuel efficiency and reduced emissions. While they certainly signify progress, neither is a viable final solution. Both come with a price and sometimes that price can rival the savings. Unintended consequences will undeniably emerge with every step forward. Perhaps if these consequences can be anticipated, improvements can be made without a system of trial and error.[8]

7.8 Daylight Saving Time (DST)

Some environmental unintended consequences occur when human actions have a direct impact on the environment. Others stem from changes in the environment, due to prior human intervention, that affect humans. This paradigm can be recognized in relation to Daylight Saving Time. Stemming from ideas hundreds of years ago, the US took action to create Daylight Saving Time over forty years ago, causing unintended ramifications that are still apparent today. This example shows how human intervention with the environment—no matter how constructive it can be—can also cause unintended consequences directly affecting humans for years to come.

Benjamin Franklin first introduced in 1784 the idea for what we know as Daylight Saving Time (DST) in his essay "An Economical Project for Diminishing the Cost of Light," proposing that the time change would save money used for expensive candles. By "springing forward" an hour in the spring, darkness comes closer to bedtime. Time is shifted in accordance with the light hours of the day so that activities can be done during the day without the need for artificial light and darkness occurs mostly while the majority of people are sleeping. DST once began on the first Sunday in April and ended on the last Sunday in October, but was lengthened in 2007 to last from the second Sunday in March through the first Sunday in November. The extension, brought about in the Energy Policy Act signed by President George W. Bush on August 8, 2005, was a response to growing energy concerns. While, just as Benjamin Franklin presumed, DST results in some energy conservation, it also has an unintended consequence.

At the inception of DST, most believed that it was a productive policy. It is unclear, though, whether they foresaw its possible consequences. Adjusting to the time changes at the beginning and end of DST has proven to be more difficult than was expected. The chief problem associated with these changes is the trouble both drivers and pedestrians have adjusting when darkness suddenly comes an hour earlier. According to professors David Gerard and Paul Fishbeck of Carnegie Mellon University, someone is almost three times as likely to be hit and killed by a motor vehicle just after DST ends as they are before the adjustment. Gerard and Fishbeck claim that the lack of light is not the problem, but the sudden change. They also found that November has by far the highest number of pedestrian deaths at 6 p.m., and that the number falls steadily through May. Another study, by John Sullivan at the University of Michigan, shows that from 1987 to 1997 pedestrian deaths jumped from 65 to 227 in the weeks before and after the end of DST, respectively.

Drivers also have a hard time adjusting to the changes in light and time but to a lesser extent than pedestrians due to "the presence of vehicle lights, which make vehicles visible to other drivers during darkness," the study by Dr. Douglas Coate and Dr. Sara Markowitz of Rutgers University (2002) states.

Because of this evidence and energy concerns, some are clamoring for year-long DST. With no need to adjust for change DST would rather prevent traffic accidents and fatalities. The already mentioned study by Coate and Markowitz predicts that year-long DST would lead to a decrease of 343 pedestrian deaths per year, or 13%, and 3% of motor vehicle occupant deaths.

While data suggests that DST saves lives, it is simultaneously the indirect cause of fatalities. If yearlong DST were instituted in the US, hundreds of lives could be saved every year.

Critical Thinking Questions

For each "case study" in the Chapter:

1. Discuss the Direction of change. For example, good intentions may lead to negative consequences; or, something positive may come up as a result of negative conditions; the consequence is neither good nor bad but a modification of the previous condition, etc.

2. Discuss the Nature of consequences—unintended, unforeseen, ironic.

3. What did go "wrong" and why? Why was the outcome unforeseen/ unintended? Was it due to ignorance, error, immediate interest, basic values, intensity of the action, etc.?

4. Discuss the Nature of an action—was it unorganized or formally organized?

Notes

1. Richards, Phillip . "Easter Bunny and the Bilby: A rabbit plague destroys pasture a native marsupial endangered." *Suite101.com* 23 Mar. 2007 http://organicgardens. suite 101.com/article.cfm/easter_bunny_and_the_bilby (accessed October 8, 2008); Bloomfield, Tim. "Rabbits and Their Impact." *Department of Primary Industries*. June 1999. The State Government of Victoria. 8 Oct. 2008 http://www.dpi.vic.gov.au/ (accessed October8, 2008)

2. Domin, Rusty. "Border-fence Dispute Snares Rare Jaguars." *CNN.com*. 5 May 2008. CNN. www.cnn.com (accessed October 8, 2008); see also Blakeslee, Sandra. "Gone for Decades, Jaguars Steal Back to the Southwest." *New York Times* 10 Oct. 2006.

3. Gaynor, Tim. "U.S. Jaguars Threatened by Mexico Border Fence." *Reuters* 25 March 2008; Hebert, H. Josef. "U.S. Jaguar Plan Foiled by Border Fence, Critics Say." *National Geographic News*. 18 Jan. 2008. National Geographic Society. www.national geographic.com (accessed October 8, 2008);

4. Carroll, Chris. "High-Tech Trash." *National Geographic* Jan. 2008: 64-81; Mayfield, Kendra. "E-Waste: Dark Side of Digital Age." *Wired.com*. 10 Jan. 2003. http://www.wired.com/science/discoveries/news/2003/01/57151 (accessed February 5, 2008).

5. Warrick, Joby. "Appalachia Is Paying Price for White House Rule Change." *Washington Post* 17 Aug. 2004.

6. "Climate Change." EPA. 1 Apr. 2008. U.S. Environmental Protection Agency. 8 Oct. 2008 http://www.epa.gov/climatechange/ accessed October 8, 2008); "Potential New Threat for Coral Reefs and Health of Communities in the Tropics." *Science Daily* 9 Sep. 2008. 8 Oct. 2008 http://www.sciencedaily.com/releases/2008/09/080904112656.htm (accessed October 8, 2008); Casey, Michael. "Seafood Poisoning Rises With Warming." *USA Today* 2 Apr. 2007.

7. Winegrad, Gerald. "Why Avian Impacts are a Concern in Wind Energy Development." *Information Bridge*. Department of Energy. http://www.osti.gov/bridge/servlets /purl/836926-JJs9me/native/836926.pdf (accessed March 1, 2008); Trent, Tiffany. "Tilting at the Appalachian Windmills." *Appalachian Voices*. Aug. 2006. http://www.app voices.org/index.php?/site/voice_storiestilting_at_the_appalachia_windmills/issue/518 (accessed March 1, 2008).

8. Williamson, Richard. "How Hybrid Cars Work." The Desert News 15 May 2003 [Salt Lake City]; "Bill Would Help Blind be Aware of Hybrids." *Los Angeles Times* 9 Apr. 2008; Motavalli, Jim. "Fear, but Few Facts, on Hybrid Risk." *The New York Times* 27 Apr. 2008; "Pros and Cons of Ethanol." *Hybrid Cars*. 27 Sep. 2006. http://www.hy bridcars.com/ethanol/benefits-drawbacks.html (accessed October 8, 2008); Nothstine, Ray. "The Unintended Consequences of the Ethanol Quick Fix." *The Christian Science Monitor* 27 July 2007; Wald, Matthew L. "Ethanol's Stock as a Fuel Source is Rising." *The New York Times* 12 June 2005.

9. Aldrich, Bob. "Saving Time, Saving Energy." *California Energy Commission*. 8 Oct. 2008 http://www.energy.ca.gov/daylightsaving.html (accessed October 8, 2008); Borenstein, Seth. "Study Ties Time Shift, Pedestrian Deaths." *USA Today* 2 Nov. 2007; Coate, Douglas, and Sara Markowitz. "Pedestrian Fatalities, Motor Vehicle Occupant Fatalities, and Daylight Saving Time." Rutgers University. May 2002. *Cornwall Center Publication Series*. 8 Oct. 2008 www.cornwall.rutgers.edu/pdf/Daylight%20Saving%20 TimeReport.pdf; Meierdierks-Lehman, Sheya. "The New Daylight Saving Time: Will it Really Work?" *Columbia News Service* 27 Feb. 2007.

Chapter 8

Crime and Crime Control. Drug Use

8.1 Cracking Down on Illegal Immigration[1]

For many years, the United States has been trying to battle the issue of illegal immigration, particularly from Mexico. Hundreds of thousands of immigrants cross the southern border illegally each year. There are a multitude of reasons that many Americans see this as a problem, including the idea that immigrants are taking their jobs away from them, or collecting welfare checks from their taxes. Although there have been numerous efforts to curb illegal immigration, nothing has seemed to make a significant difference thus far. In an issue of LA Weekly, Marc Cooper (2003) explores how measures to stop this immigration have helped—but more specifically hurt—the efforts to end the turbulent situation at the border.

This analysis goes into not one action, but many actions performed by everyone from the federal and state governments to vigilante border-watchers. All of these actions were intentionally completed in order to achieve this purpose to stop illegal immigration from Mexico. One action is the concentration of border guards around certain areas that were once overwhelmed with illegal immigrants trying to cross the border. These four areas—located around San Diego, CA; El Paso, TX; Brownsville, TX; and the central Arizona border—are well-guarded. Although the goal of stopping illegal traffic at these points has been achieved, this fortification leads to another unintended problem: because Mexican immigrants are forced away from the heavily-fortified areas, they are forced to make difficult journeys through unsafe conditions. Many immigrants die trying to reach the U.S. of sunstroke or dehydration in the desert or freezing temperatures in the mountains. According to Wayne Cornelius, director of the Center for Comparative Immigration Studies at the University of California, San Diego,

"The U.S.-Mexican border has been 10 times deadlier to Mexican immigrants in the last 10 years than was the whole 28-year history of the Berlin Wall [to East Germans]." It is debatable, however, that this consequence is viewed as negative or unintended to those responsible for securing the border. If illegal immigrants die trying to reach America without ever interacting with border guards, the blood is not on America's hands. The supposed intent of concentrating border security was to deter Mexicans from trying to illegally immigrate because conditions at other parts of the border are so dangerous. But perhaps it is just as easy to make the claim that the death toll of illegal immigrants is another way of lowering the number entering the U.S., no matter how ethically or morally reprehensible it may be.

There is another unintended consequence of the border policy which is possibly much more disturbing to policy-makers. As many Mexican illegal immigrants cross the border to earn income and then return to their country to help support their family until they must go back and work again, there is a continuous cycle of immigration and emigration between the two countries. Not only has the terrain deterred (or killed) illegal *immigrants*, it has also deterred illegal *emigrants*, meaning that it is increasing the number of them living in the United States, scared or unable to return to Mexico.

To reach the United States without having to endure harsh conditions and possibly death, many Mexicans choose to pay someone to transport them across the border illegally. These human smugglers, known as "polleros" or "coyotes," have increased in popularity, and increased their prices. Undoubtedly, the increase of funds puts much more power in the hands of these criminals, who also often transport narcotics to the U.S. Drug and human smugglers naturally lead to an increase of crime, particularly drug crime in the Southwest and have become a large problem for locals there, including those living on Arizona's Tohono O'odham Indian reservation. According to Cooper's article, deaths around the reservation rose over 1,100% between 1995 and 2000 and drug trafficking is an increasing problem as well. Corruption has taken many of the Indians, who are few in numbers. With all of these problems stemming from seemingly insufficient/ineffective border policy, one might think that the federal government would see an urgency to step in and make a change more significant than the building of a fence. But, Claudia Smith, public-interest lawyer and immigration policy critic, maintains that they have no plans to do so. She says: "Welcome to the border of hypocrisy. The U.S. never intended to fully close the border, they just wanted to keep (illegal) immigration out of the public eye."

However discouraging Smith's words may be, the realities of the unintended consequences of American border policy seem to back up her statement. Public outcry is constant in the Southwest and the negative consequences of illegal immigration are actively publicized by the media. Several groups of citizens have decided to use their own resources to combat what they see as a major problem threatening the United States because they too feel that their federal government has failed them. This is, arguably, another negative unintended consequence of the concentration of strict border policy in certain areas—the lack of oversight in others. These vigilantes and militiamen carry guns and often mistaken views of what most illegal immigrants are actually coming to America to do. These "guards" claim to be peaceful and that they are there only to notify Border Patrol of problems along the border, but there is no oversight of what exactly they are doing because there is no one on the border. According to Cooper's article, the Mexican government has complained to the U.S. about the militiamen and that Border Patrol has denied that they want or need the assistance. The question of whether more people are needed is certainly up for debate, but the statement from the patrol had no effect on the attitudes of these vigilantes, who still remain on the border.

One of the most stunning facts that Cooper points out in his article is the readiness of the woman under whose authority the current border policy was implemented to admit how ineffective it is. Doris Meissner, former commissioner of the Immigration and Naturalization Service, agrees that decisions were made out of necessity, to get the border problem taken care of as quickly as possible. Her comments make it obvious that Merton's theory of "imperious immediacy of interest" was a huge factor in the unintended consequences of America's border policy (Merton 1936).[2] Meissner describes how important the issue was at the time and says that the first time she met with Janet Reno, Reno said "You will do the border first." Meissner agrees that the death toll of Mexican illegal immigrants is unreasonable and that something needs to be done. "The huge paradox now is that the unintended consequences far overshadow the positive," she said.

8.2 Megan's Law

In 1996, Megan Kanka was murdered by a sex offender in New Jersey. Immediately following the murder, Megan's Law was passed. The law elaborates on the 1994 Jacob Wetterling Crimes Against Children and Sexually Violent Offender Registration Act, which required al sex offenders to be registered with and tracked by law enforcement. Megan's Law made this registry public. The law was meant to address the issue of sex offenders as a threat to communities who do not know their identity. It was intended to safeguard the lives of citizens against dangerous offenders. Unfortunately, this has not been the result thus far.

By 2003, sex offender registries were required to be posted online in all 50 states. While approximately half of the states present information classifying the threat level an offender poses, many do not. This has proven to be problematic. While common perceptions of sexual offenders are that they are all dangerous and unable to be rehabilitated, this is not true. Sex offender registries, for instance, list people who have been convicted of crimes such as being in a consensual sexual relationship with a partner a few years younger when they were teenagers. The psychological effect on these individuals stemming from being a registered sex offender is only one negative effect of Megan's Law.

Without classifying sexual offenders by the threat they pose to a community, they are blanketed under the same terrible label.

According to data presented by Dr. Jill Levenson in *Behavioral Sciences and the Law* in 2007, virtually no evidence has been found the Megan's Law reduces recidivism of sex offenders, makes arrests easier, or keeps communities safer. In fact, the negative unanticipated consequences of Megan's Law fall on the offenders themselves, and are often passed on to the community.

According to Levenson, "a large majority of health professionals have expressed doubt that registration and notification can be successful in preventing child sexual abuse, and even speculated that such laws create a false sense of security for parents." Rehabilitation is possible, but only through social reintegration. By being placed on internet offender registries, offenders are often denied housing, employment, and stable family lives. They are often harassed, assaulted, and threatened. Often unable to support themselves without reliable employment, they may be lured into criminal acts to support themselves—facilitating recidivism in one way.

Levenson studied groups of registered offenders to understand their opinions about Megan's Law. While many were not opposed to it, a significant majority noted that it had made their lives extremely difficult. Experiencing isolation, depression, harassment, and emotional instability, offenders find it impossible to reintegrate into society to rehabilitate themselves. Without the opportunity for less dangerous offenders to be recognized as such on online registries, they are assumed to be a dangerous criminal that many of them are not. By ostracizing them and advertising their crimes, offenders are forced to live lives that are not conducive to recovery or change. Without significant positive advantages for law enforcement empowered by Megan's Law, the positive consequences of internet sex offender registry have not been seen. Negative unintended consequences such as recidivism, mental anguish, and lack of productivity have thus far outweighed the prospect of positive ramifications.[3]

8.3 Legalizing Abortion

From 1993 to 2000 serious crime was falling steadily to the lowest level in a quarter century. Robbery was at rates last achieved in the 1960s, murder has declined a third since 1993 and reached the levels not seen in more than three decades.

There are numerous alternative theories of why crime has declined so swiftly and steeply. One is about booming economy, whose benefits were trickling even to the poor and undereducated. Another is about longer prison sentences and record incarceration rates. With nearly two million convicts behind bars, America is home to a quarter of the world's prison inmates, and that's not counting 4 million plus who are on probation or parole. It might be also due to a declining popularity of crack; to smarter policing; increased number of new cops on the nation's streets. Demography may also play a role in a sense of fewer adolescents and young men in their peak crime years. Or is it a cyclical effect of a rise and fall? According to a report released in 1999 by two leading economists, the University of Chicago's Steven D. Levitt and John J. Donohue III of

Stanford Law School, the nation's crime drop is the result of an increase in abortions following the Supreme Court's 1973 decision establishing a constitutional right to the procedure. Fewer crimes are being committed now, the authors concluded, because many unwanted children who might have grown up in bad households and in conditions that often lead to criminal lives were never born. "Interestingly, it was 19 years after the abortion ruling—which would have put the generation-that-wasn't in the midst of the high-crime years—that crime began its rather steep descent" (Fletcher 2000).[4]

8.4 Amendment 18 (1919) and Alcohol Prohibition

Before the prohibition of alcohol existed in the United States people freely drank alcohol, mainly beer, some responsibly and some irresponsibly. The government was able to collect quite a substantial amount of tax revenue for the manufacture, transportation, sales, and consumption of alcohol. In the years leading up to the prohibition of alcohol the rates of serious and alcohol consumption were steadily dropping, they rose during the mid-latter yeas of prohibition. There were relatively small numbers of prisoners throughout the United States, especially in federal prisons, which wasn't much of a tax burden on the public. People generally drank responsibly, but there was a growing puritanical movement in the United States that found drinking alcohol for the purpose of intoxication morally reprehensible.

Alcohol was outlawed to attempt to decrease deviant social behavior as well as criminal behavior so they figured it they got rid of alcohol there would be less crime, less dependence on addictive substances, less prisoners and less of a tax burden. The Eighteenth Amendment was certified January 29, 1919 and thus began the years of the alcohol prohibition.

The manufacture, sale, or transportation of intoxicating liquors within, the importation thereof into, or the exportation from the United States and all territory became prohibited. The Congress and the several States received concurrent power to enforce this law by appropriate legislation

There are many unintended consequences related to the prohibition of alcohol, they can be broken down into two different categories: the exact opposite of what the amendment was supposed to do, and also unforeseen consequences.

While the crime rate was generally decreasing into the prohibition it began to steadily rise during prohibition, common crimes stayed even or somewhat decreased, but serious crimes were more prevalent. The homicide rate in large cities increased from 5.6 per 100,000 population during the first decade of the century to 8.4 during the second decade when the Harrison Narcotics Act, a 3wave of state alcohol prohibitions, and World War I alcohol restrictions were enacted. The homicide rate increased to 10 per 100,000 population during the 1920s, a 78 percent increase over the pre-Prohibition period. The Volstead Act, passed to enforce the Eighteenth Amendment, had an immediate impact on crime. According to a study of 30 major U.S. cities, the number of crimes increased 24 percent between 1920 and 1921. Arrests for drunkenness and disorderly conduct increased 41 percent, and arrests of drunken drivers increased 81 percent. Among crimes with victims, thefts and burglaries increased 9 percent, while homicides and incidents of assault and battery increased 13 percent.

The prohibition of alcohol also led to a new breed of very organized crime syndicates. They controlled the business of alcohol, which led to other legal and illegal business ventures. Some of the most idolized criminals ever were born out of the mafia alcohol smuggling era of prohibition. They controlled supply and demand and they controlled the price, and they reaped the benefits. A big problem with the level of organization of the crime groups was the level of corruption among officials and law enforcement. A lot of deferent people were making money from illegal booze.

Also as crime rates rose, the rate of prisoners climbed as well, which would be the exact opposite of the intended consequence of lowering the rates of crime and prisoners. Before Prohibition and the Harrison Narcotics Act (1914), there had been 400 federal convicts, fewer than 3,000 of whom were housed in federal prisons. By 1932 the number of federal convicts had increased 561 percent, to 26,589, and the federal prison population had increased 366 percent. Much of the increase was due to violations of the Volstead Act and other Prohibition laws. The number of people convicted of Prohibition violations increased 1,000 percent between 1925 and 1930, and fully half of all prisoners received in 1930 had been convicted of alcohol and drug offences, and that figure rises to 75 percent of violators if other commercial prohibitions were included. In 1921, 95.933 illicit distilleries, stills, still works and fermentors were seized. In 1925, the total jumped to 172,537 and up to 282,122 in 1930. In connection with these seizures, 34,175 persons were arrested in 1921; by 1925, the number had risen to 62,747 and to a high in 1928 of 75,307. This also had the affect of becoming a tax burden (that still exists to this day!), keeping all of those prisoners becomes expensive. Total federal expenditures on penal institutions increased more than 1,000 percent between 1915 and 1932. Because of the excessive amount of drug related inmates prisons are also overcrowded. The increase cost of law enforcement to combat the smuggling and bootlegging of alcohol, and other alcohol or organized crime related shenanigans was also a tax burden. This was a double negative considering the lost tax revenue from the sales of alcohol and establishments that served alcohol due to prohibition. The court system was also constantly clogged with alcohol related crimes, which takes resources away from more serious crimes.

When people can't have something they tend to amp up the power when they are able to get it. People began drinking harder alcohol and largely gave up on beer when prohibition happened, people figure they have to get more bang for their buck or make it worth the risk. Not only did people begin drinking more powerful drinks, the drinks became more potent overall, the moonshine that bootleggers were making was much more potent than liquor had been before it was proclaimed illegal. Moonshine to this day is still the most powerful thing you can find to drink. Sometimes the people making the illegal liquor didn't know what they were doing and the substance could be harmful to the consumer, there was more of a danger or chance of injury with unregulated alcohol. As stated by the pro-prohibition economist Irving Fisher, "I am credibly

> informed that a very conservative reckoning would set the poisonous effects of bootleg beverages as compared with medicinal liquors at ten to one; that is, it requires only a tenth as much bootleg liquor as pre-prohibition liquor to produce a given degree of drunkenness. The reason, of course, is that bootleg liquor is so concentrated and almost invariably contains other and more deadly poisons that mere ethyl alcohol."

In 1925 the death rate from poisoned liquor was 4,154 as compared to 1,604 in 1920.

When alcohol was legal, the government was able to regulate who received a license and where they could operate a business that served alcohol. While alcohol is illegal then the government is largely unable to monitor illegal activity, they are unable to control who is serving alcohol, who they are serving alcohol to, and where they are operating their business. They couldn't monitor the type of alcohol they were serving. This also led to other illegal activities such as prostitution and gambling, people figured they were already breaking the law, they might as well go big. People also moved to harder less regulated drugs once alcohol was outlawed.

On a more inspiring note prohibition also spawned the beginnings of American stock car racing. Stock car racing in the United States has its origins in bootlegging during Prohibition, when drivers ran bootleg whiskey made in Appalachia. Bootleggers needed to distribute their illicit products, and they typically used small, fast vehicles to better evade the police. Many of the drivers would modify their cars for speed and handling, as well as increased cargo capacity, and some of them came to love the fast-paced driving down twisty mountain roads.

Amendment 18 is the only constitutional amendment to be repealed. The major consequence of any type of prohibition of a substance is going to be an increase in crime, and specifically violent crime. Prohibition leads to organized crime, gang related murder, extortion, and corruption. Prohibition also drastically reduces the government control of a substance, which leads to a more dangerous product, a loss of tax dollars, and a black market which also leads to a more dangerous product, a further loss of tax dollars and a black market which also leads to the above mentioned serious crimes. Prohibition or new laws also causes a severe increase in prisoners, and a huge tax burden that we could do without.

8.5 The "Three Strikes" Law

In the 1980s, violent crime rate was rising. As a response to popular demands, the politicians passed the "three strikes" law. Anyone who is convicted of a third felony receives an automatic mandatory sentence. Judges are not allowed to consider the circumstances. Some mandatory sentences carry life imprisonment. The law did not limit the punishment to violent crimes and it did not differentiate between types of felonies. James Henslin's Sociology textbook reviews some real life cases as consequences of the law.

In Los Angeles, a twenty-seven year old man was sentenced to twenty five years for stealing a pizza. In New York City, a man who was about to be sentenced for selling crack said to the judge, "I'm only 19. This is terrible." He then hurled himself out of a courtroom window, plunging to his death sixteen stories below. In Sacramento, a man who passed himself off as Tiger Woods to go on a $17,000 shopping spree, was sentenced to two hundred years in prison. In California, a man who stole 9 videotapes from Kmart was sentenced to 50 years in prison without parole. He appealed to the U.S. Supreme Court, which upheld his sentence. In Utah, a twenty-five year old was sentenced to fifty five years in prison for selling small bags of marijuana to a police informant.[6]

Critical Thinking Questions

For each "case study" in the Chapter:

1. Discuss the Direction of change. For example, good intentions may lead to negative consequences; or, something positive may come up as a result of negative conditions; the consequence is neither good nor bad but a modification of the previous condition, etc.

2. Discuss the Nature of consequences—unintended, unforeseen, ironic.

3. What did go "wrong" and why? Why was the outcome unforeseen/ unintended? Was it due to ignorance, error, immediate interest, basic values, intensity of the action, etc.?

4. Discuss the Nature of an action—was it unorganized or formally organized?

Notes

1. This part is based on Cooper, Marc. "On the Border of Hypocrisy: The Unintended Consequences of Getting Tough on Illegal Immigration." *LA Weekly*, 5 December 2003.

2. Merton, Robert K. "The Unanticipated Consequences of Purposive Social Action." *American Sociological Review* 1 (December 1936): 894-904.

3. Levenson, Jill S. "Megan's Law and its IMpact on Community Re-entry for Sex Offenders." Wiley Interscience. 9 July 2007. *Behavioral Sciences and the Law*. (accessed

15 Apr. 2008); "Sex Offender Laws Have Unintended Consequence" Minnesota Public Radio. 18 June 2007.

4. Fletcher, Michael A. "The Crime Conundrum." *The Washington Post*, Sunday, January 16, 2000, F1-F5.

5. See http://www.Cato.org/pub_display.php?pub_id=1017&full=1; http://en.wikipediaorgwiki/NASCAR; http://en.wikipedia.org/wikiEighteenth_Amendment_to_the_United_States_Constitution; http://druglibrary.org/schaffer/library/basicfax.htm

6. Henslin, James M. *Sociology. A down-to-Earth Approach*. 8th edition. (Pearson, 2007); see also Cloud, John 1998. "For Better or Worse." *Time*, October 26, 1998, 43-44; Reuters, "Fake Tiger Woods Gets 200-Years-To-Life in Prison," April 28, 2001; Greenhouse, Linda 2003. "Justices Uphold Long Prison Terms in Repeat Crimes." *New York Times*, March 6, 2003; Madigan, Nick "Judge Questions Long Sentence in Drug Case." *New York Times*, November 17, 2004.

Chapter 9

Conclusion. Looking Down the Road

Feather adornments, including helmets, capes and cloaks, god images, and lei, were very important in traditional (before 1800) Hawaiian society for use as emblems and symbols of rank and status. The seven endemic birds were considered as the most desirable for these purposes. There is also evidence that the bird feathers were used as prestige goods to build alliances and as money. The bird-catches, usually men, represented a special class in society and had their own patron deities. The endemic birds, however, were not killed. The bird-catches knew exactly how many feathers could be plugged out from the bird to let it live and grow new feathers.[1] The Hawaiians were perfectly aware that with a potential disappearance of birds, their social, political, and economic life would be tremendously distorted.

This Hawaiian practice is an excellent example of what has been defined almost two hundred years later—sustainable development. In 1987, the United Nations World Commission on Environment and Development coined this term as "development that meets the needs of the present without compromising the ability of future generations to meet their own needs." The idea is that somehow we will be able to find the magical formula whereby everybody is better off in the future and we can all live happily ever after.[2]

It seems that the topic of unintended consequences is in the air, so to speak, in theory and in practice.

Several authors wrote recently about different aspects of "unintended consequences." Steven D. Levitt and Stephen J. Dubner in their *Freakonomics* (2005) explore, as economists, "the hidden side of everything." Its central idea is: if morality represents how people would like the world to work, then economics shows how it actually does work. As a step further, behavioral economics, an increasingly popular field that incorporates elements from psychology attempts to explain *why* people make seemingly irrational decisions.

In *The Moral Consequences of Economic Growth; Day of Reckoning: The Consequences of American Economic Policy* (1988) Benjamin Friedman illustrates how rising incomes render a society more open and democratic. He makes clear that growth, rather than just the level of living standards is key to effecting political and social liberalization in the third world. But the next twenty years demonstrated exclusionary consequences of "development." For example, the *Contesting Development: Critical Struggles for Social Change* (2010) edited by Philip McMichael is a collection of case studies to reveal the limiting assumptions of development.[3]

The unintended consequences of technology are, probably, explored best[4] and for that reason we did not devote a separate chapter to this topic. Charles Handy in *The Age of Unreason* (1990) claims that technologies can have fundamental effects on the way we live. According to Handy, microwave ovens were a clever idea, but

> their inventor could hardly have realized that their effect would ultimately be to take the preparation of food out of the home and into the, increasingly automated, factory; to make cooking as it used to be into a matter of choice, not of necessity; to alter the habits of our homes, making the dining table outmoded for many, as each member of the family individually heats up his or her own meal as and when they require it.

In *Why Things Bite Back: Technology and the Revenge of Unintended Consequences* (1996) Edward Tenner sees in some of our technologies a "revenge effect" in which our perverse technologies turn against us with consequences which exceed the good which had been planned. For example, security

> is another window on revenge effects. Power door locks, now standard on most cars, increase the sense of safety. But they have helped triple or quadruple the number of drivers locked out over the last two decades—costing $400 million a year and exposing drivers to the very criminals the locks were supposed to defeat.

The publication by Greg Perry *America: The Unintended Consequences of the Government's Protection of the Handicapped* (2004), to which we refer in Chapter 5, documents the unintended and for the most part negative consequences of the government's actions to offer equal employment opportunities to the Americans with Disabilities. *Irony in the Work of Philosophy* (2002) by Claire Colebrook, looks at the literary tradition of irony and its development in modernism into free-indirect style.[5]

In their daily practices people are increasingly looking down the road. The trend of 'segmented assimilation" (Alejandro Portes; Patricia Fernandez-Kelly) is largely due to increased people's willingness to consider pros and cons of full cultural assimilation.

Jobyina Caldwell, assistant superintendent for Virginia Beach high schools, is also willing to look at the research by Robert Verona. Dr. Robert Verona studied DMV records and found Chesapeake teens, who start school around 8:40 in the morning had far fewer crashes than Virginia Beach teens who start at 7:20. The crash rate in Virginia Beach was 1.4 times greater than the crash rate in teens in Chesapeake. Verona believes the teens who start school later may be more alert. Previous sleep studies show teens need about nine hours. But just because Chesapeake schools start later does not guarantee teens in that city are sleeping longer. Verona's study did not look at that, nor driving distances and roadway congestion. Dr. Verona admits that his research alone is not proof, but he is planning future studies, and hopes to one day prevent more car accidents by getting schools to start later.

Nina Bernstein, the New York Times correspondent, implies that the actions of immigration services were perfectly intended while not stated specifically (2010). In February 2010, federal authorities shut down New York City's only immigration detention center, and sent most of its detainees to a county jail in New Jersey. Obama administration officials stressed that the jail was only a short drive from the city.

> But under a contract with a private telephone company, calls to detainees' families and lawyers back in New York are decidedly long distance. The result is a 800 percent increase in the cost of a call, to more than 89 cents a minute, in a phone system so cumbersome that detainees say it impedes their ability to contest deportation or contact relatives.

The calls from the New Jersey county jails are charged at rates negotiated by the state and the phone provider, Global Tel Link of Reston, Va. The rate is $1.75 to connect a call, and 89 cents a minute. But Global Tel Link will not connect a call until the recipient puts $25 into an account with a major credit card. Many lawyers will not accept such calls, and many family members do not have a credit card, said Karen Grisez, chairwoman of the bar association's commission on immigration. Typically, phone companies compete not to provide more reasonable rates to inmates and their families, but to provide the highest commissions to the jail. Dorothy Cukier, a spokeswoman for Global Tel Link, said it was not the company's responsibility to negotiate special rates for immigration detainees.

As the consequence of the transfer, the possibility for communication with the outside world have shrunk. If further isolation of many immigration detainees was not an intended action on the side of local authorities, then, how to explain many similar grievances? In their complaints, detainees said they were not even allowed to read newspapers or watch the news. "They stop us from knowing what is going on with our own family and around us," one letter said.[6]

In summer of 2005, the Food and Drug Administration (FDA) has approved BiDil—a combination drug designed to restore low or depleted nitric oxide levels to the blood to treat or prevent cases of congestive heart failure. The manufacture originally intended the drug for the general population, and race was irrelevant. "In a remarkable turn of events, however, BiDil was reborn as a racialized intervention. One of the investigators reviewed the data and found that African Americans in the original clinical trial seemed to show better outcomes than whites" (Duster 2005/2006).[7] The most obvious unintended consequence of FDA approving a new drug designed for African Americans, then, seems to be that the action calls into question whether or not there are genetic differences between people of different racial and ethnic backgrounds. It has not been proven, however, that there is any scientific basis for this assumption. It carries with it the dangerous possibility of legitimizing prejudices and discrimination of minorities based on the idea that it is a fact that these minority group members are genetically different—and possibly genetically inferior—to dominant group members. In his Presidential Address to the centennial meeting of the American Sociological Association (2005) Troy Duster appealed to the audience:

> Sociologists can stand on the sidelines, watch the parade of reductionist science as it goes by, and point out that it is all "socially constructed". That will not be good enough to rain on this parade, because of the imprimatur of legitimacy increasingly afforded to the study of so-called basic processes inside the body.

Rather, sociologists should explore, from a variety of angles, where the production of racial drugs may take us down the road.

Notes

1. Emerson Nathaniel B. *The bird-hunters of ancient Hawaii.* (Hawaiian almanac and annual for 1895. Thos. G. Thrum, compiler and publisher, Honolulu, 1894); see also: Ermolaeva, Elena. *Chiefdom to State: Cultural Identity and Hierarchy formation in the Ancient Hawaiian World-System.* (Unpublished Ph.D. dissertation, The Johns Hopkins University, 1997).

2. *Our Common Future* (World Commission on Environment and Development, New York: Oxford University Press, 1987); see also Weeks, John R. *Population. An Introduction to Concepts and Issues.* 9th edition, (Wadsworth, 2005).

3. Steven D. Levitt and Stephen J. Dubner. *Freakonomics.* (Harper Collins Publishers, 2005); Loewenstein, George and Peter Ubel. "Economics Behaving Badly." New York Times, July 14, 2010 http:www.nytimes.com (accessed July 15, 2010); Friedman, Benjamin. *The Moral Consequences of Economic Growth; Day of Reckoning: The Consequences of American Economic Policy Under Reagan and After* (New York: Random House, 1988); *Contesting Development: Critical Struggles for Social Change,* edited by Philip McMichael. (Routledge; 2010)

4. See Handy, Charles. *The Age of Unreason.* (Harvard Business School Press, Boston, 1990); Tenner, Edward. *Why Things Bite Back: Technology and the Revenge of Unintended Consequences.* (Alfred a Knopf Inc., 1996).

5. Perry, Greg. *Disabling America: The Unintended Consequences of the Government's Protection of the Handicapped* (Nelson Current, 2004); Colebrook, Claire. *Irony in the Work of Philosophy* (University of Nebraska Press, 2002).

6. *Later school days may prevent crashes.* NBC, June 10, 2010 http://www.msnbc.msn.com/id/37602709 (accessed June 10, 2010); Bernstein, Nina. "Move Further Isolates Immigration detainees." *New York Times*, A23, March 17, 2010.

7. Troy, Duster. "Comparative Perspectives and Competing Explanations: Taking on the Newly Configured Reductionist Challenge to Sociology." (2005 Presidential Address. *American Sociological Review*, 2006, Vol. 71 February, pp. 1-15); see also Kahn, J. "Harmonizing Race: Competing Regulatory Paradigms of Racial Categorization in International Drug Development." *Santa Clara Journal of International Law*, 2006, pp. 34-56.

About the Authors

Elena Ermolaeva, Ph.D. is an Associate Professor in the Department of Sociology/Anthropology at Marshall University. She is an international sociologist with more than thirty four years of professional experience.

Jessica Ross is an undergraduate student in the Department of Sociology/Anthropology at Marshall University.